D0597802

Better Homes and Gardens®

WOOD™

ROUTER TECHNIQUES

AND PROJECTS YOU CAN MAKE

WE CARE!

All of us at Meredith® Books are dedicated to giving you the
information and ideas you need to create beautiful and useful
woodworking projects. We guarantee your satisfaction with this
book for as long as you own it. We also welcome your comments
and suggestions. Please write us at Meredith® Books, BB-117,
1100 Walnut St., Des Moines, IA 50309-3400.

© Copyright 1993 by Meredith Corporation, Des Moines, Iowa. All Rights Reserved. Printed in the United States of America.
First Edition. Printing Number and Year: 5 4 3 2   97 96 95 94
Library of Congress Catalog Card Number: 92-81777. ISBN: 0-696-02473-X.

A WOOD™ BOOK
Published by Meredith® Books

MEREDITH® BOOKS
President, Book Group: Joseph J. Ward
Vice President and Editorial Director: Elizabeth P. Rice
Executive Editor: Connie Schrader
Art Director: Ernest Shelton
Prepress Production Manager: Randall Yontz

WOOD® MAGAZINE
President, Magazine Group: William T. Kerr
Editor: Larry Clayton

ROUTER TECHNIQUES AND PROJECTS YOU CAN MAKE
Produced by Roundtable Press, Inc.
Directors: Susan E. Meyer, Marsha Melnick
Senior Editor: Sue Heinemann
Managing Editor: Ross L. Horowitz
Graphic Designer: Leah Lococo
Design Assistant: Leslie Goldman
Art Assistant: Ahmad Mallah
Copy Assistant: Amy Handy

For Meredith® Books
Editorial Project Manager/Assistant Art Director: Tom Wegner
Contributing How-To Editors: Marlen Kemmet,
    Charles E. Sommers
Contributing Techniques Editor: Bill Krier
Contributing Tool Editor: Larry Johnston
Contributing Outline Editor: David A. Kirchner

Special thanks to Khristy Benoit

Meredith Corporation Corporate Officers:
Chairman of the Executive Committee: E. T. Meredith III
Chairman of the Board, President and Chief Executive
    Officer:
    Jack D. Rehm
Group Presidents: Joseph J. Ward, Books; William T. Kerr,
    Magazines; Philip A. Jones, Broadcasting; Allen L. Sabbag,
    Real Estate
Vice Presidents: Leo R. Armatis, Corporate Relations;
    Thomas G. Fisher, General Counsel and Secretary;
    Larry D. Hartsook, Finance; Michael A. Sell, Treasurer;
    Kathleen J. Zehr, Controller and Assistant Secretary

On the front cover: Musical Tone Box, pages 82–85
On the back cover, top right: Tambouriffic Rolltop Recipe
    Box, pages 86–89; bottom right: Stylized Meat Carving
    Board, pages 74–77

ROUTER TOOLS AND JIGS 4

HEAVY-DUTY ROUTER TABLE 5

HOW YOUR CHOICE OF ROUTER BITS SHAPES UP 12

HOW TO DODGE ROUTER BURNS 15

ROUTER STRAIGHTEDGE MAKES DADOES AND EDGE-JOINTING A SNAP 16

ROUTER TIPS AND TECHNIQUES 18

ROUTER BASICS 19

FIVE GREAT ROUTER TRICKS 20

BASIC MORTISE AND TENON JOINERY 26

TEMPLATE ROUTING 32

MAKE 'EM YOURSELF MOLDINGS 38

TAMBOUR 44

ROUTER PROJECTS 50

PICTURE-PERFECT PARSONS TABLE 51

CHRISTMAS-TREE TRAY 59

TEA-FOR-TWO HUTCH 63

MANCALA MARBLE GAME 68

RESPLENDENT PENDANT 72

STYLIZED MEAT CARVING BOARD 74

LAZY SUSAN 78

MUSICAL TONE BOX 82

TAMBOURIFFIC ROLLTOP RECIPE BOX 86

PLANE PERPLEXING 90

ROUTER TOOLS
AND JIGS

To help you with router projects, you can build the heavy-duty
router table and the router straightedge featured in this section.
There is also useful advice on choosing router bits as well as
avoiding router burns.

HEAVY-DUTY ROUTER TABLE

When it comes to designing workshop tools, you'd be hard pressed to find a better team than Jim Downing, *WOOD*® magazine's design editor, and Jim Boelling, the project builder. They knew that for large projects, woodworkers needed a heavy-duty router table with more horsepower, more work surface, and more dust collection capabilities than a tabletop version offered. We built and tested several prototypes until we decided on this workhorse. This hefty, professional-quality router table houses a 3hp electronic plunge router that complements the ever-increasing variety of ½"-shanked router bits on the market. It boasts a 24×36" work surface and employs two vacuum pickups for a cough-free workshop. And, after you drill mounting holes, you can attach the pin-routing attachment shown *above right*. (For instructions on building this attachment, see page 75.)

Features everywhere... just take a look!

To install and remove the router from the rabbeted opening in the router table, replace your router's subbase with a large clear acrylic **router plate** (see the Buying Guide on *page 11* for our source). The replacement plate also acts as a base when using the router away from the router table. This prevents

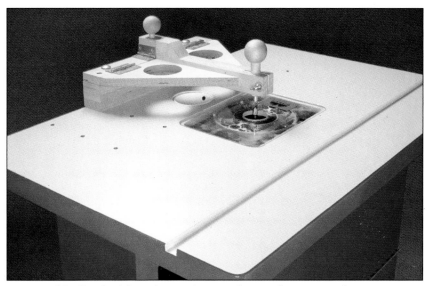

Router table fitted with a pin-routing attachment (see page 75).

you from having to change bases every time you hold the router by hand for machining operations.

To keep your shop clean and your lungs happy, connect your vacuum hose to the **upper vacuum pipe** when using the **guard** for operations such as edge molding and rabbeting. In addition, the guard helps to protect the operator from the cutter and flying chips. When you can't use the guard for operations such as dadoing, grooving, and pin routing, switch to the **lower vacuum pipe** to remove dust from below the table and bit. (A dust-free router also lasts longer.)

Attach and align the **split fences** on either side of the guard for plenty of support when routing long pieces. Offset the fences when removing stock from the entire

edge of a project. If you don't have a jointer, mount a straight bit to the router, offset the fences slightly, and joint the edges of stock.

Although you could install almost any router in this table, we chose a **3hp electronic plunge model**. In addition to driving your current supply of ¼" bits, this router handles the variety of power-hungry ½"-diameter shanked bits with ease. The electronic **speed control** on the Ryobi router we used works great to lower the speed for larger bits. We liked the

continued

HEAVY-DUTY ROUTER TABLE

continued

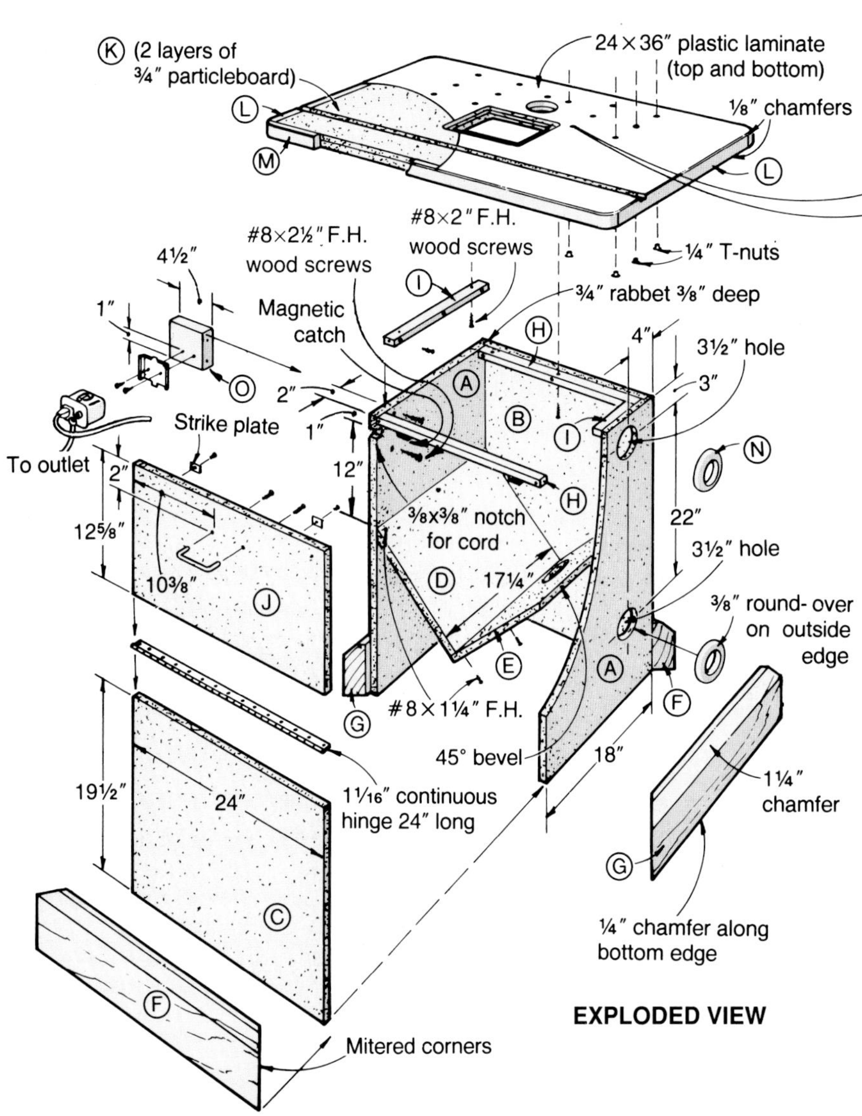
(K) (2 layers of
3/4" particleboard)
24×36" plastic laminate
(top and bottom)
1/8" chamfers
L
M
L
#8×2" F.H.
wood screws
#8×2½" F.H.
wood screws
1/4" T-nuts
3/4" rabbet 3/8" deep
4½"
1"
Magnetic
catch
I
H
4"
3½" hole
3"
O
2"
Strike plate
1"
A
B
I
N
To outlet
2"
12"
12⅝"
10⅜"
J
3/8x3/8" notch
for cord
H
22"
D
17¼"
3½" hole
3/8" round- over
on outside
edge
E
A
F
#8×1¼" F.H.
G
45° bevel
18"
1¼"
chamfer
19½"
24"
1 1/16" continuous
hinge 24" long
G
C
1/4" chamfer along
bottom edge
F
EXPLODED VIEW
Mitered corners

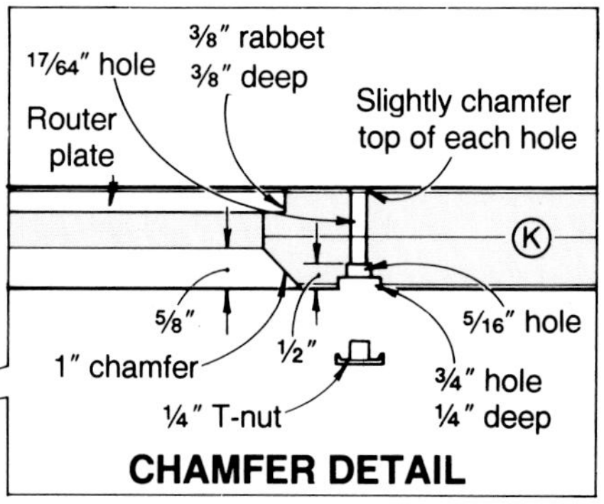
17/64" hole
3/8" rabbet
3/8" deep
Router
plate
Slightly chamfer
top of each hole
K
5/8"
1/2"
5/16" hole
1" chamfer
3/4" hole
1/4" deep
1/4" T-nut
CHAMFER DETAIL

Ryobi's **depth-control knob** for ease in raising and lowering the bit. If you already have a large router, see the Buying Guide for our source of auxiliary depth controls.

First, attach the acrylic plate to the router

Note: *To mount the router to the router table you'll need a piece of ⅜" acrylic. You can buy a piece locally, or see the Buying Guide for our source of precut plates.*

1. Remove the subbase from your router. Center and secure the ⅜" acrylic plate to your tool. Locate and scribe the mounting-hole centerpoints on the plate. Remove the plate from the router, and drill and countersink the holes to size.

2. Attach the router plate to your router. If you need longer screws to fasten the plate, our router-plate supplier can provide them. See the Buying Guide for details.

3. Chuck a ¼" straight bit into your router, and slowly plunge the bit through the plate. Remove the plate from the router, and use a circle cutter to cut a hole, centered over the ¼" routed hole, large enough to accommodate your biggest bit (our hole measures 2" in diameter).

Construction begins with the base cabinet

1. Cut the two side panels (A), back (B), and front (C) to the sizes listed in the Bill of Materials *opposite* from ¾"-thick particleboard.

2. Cut a ¾" rabbet ⅜" deep along the back edge of each side panel.

3. Glue and clamp the back into the rabbet and between the side panels. Clamp the front panel to the front of the side panels, checking for square. After the glue dries, remove the clamps and sand the joints.

4. Cut the trough sides (D, E) to size, bevel-ripping the top edge of each at 45°. Using the Top View drawing *below* for reference, mark the vacuum-hole centerpoint on the right-hand trough side (E). Mark the 3½" hole with a compass. Cut the hole to size with a jigsaw. Referring to the dimensions on the Exploded View drawing at *left*, mark the locations, and saw a pair of vacuum holes in the cabinet side (A).

5. Cut the base-surround parts (F, G) to size plus 2" in length.

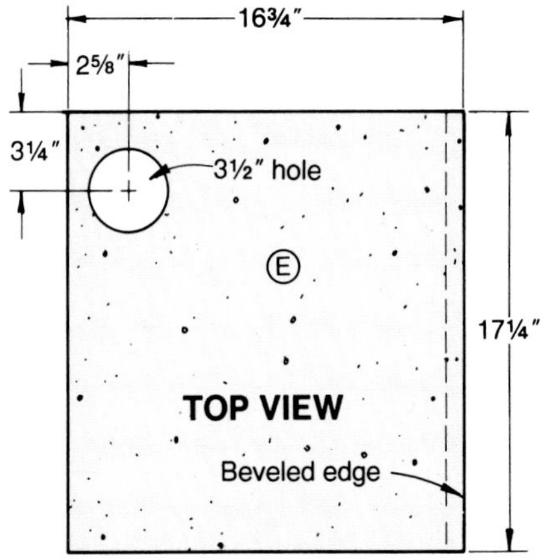
16¾"
2⅝"
3¼"
3½" hole
E
17¼"
TOP VIEW
Beveled edge

Bill of Materials

Parts	Finished Size*			Mat.	Qty.
	T	W	L		
BASE CABINET					
A sides	¾"	18"	32½"	PB	2
B back	¾"	23¼"	32½"	PB	1
C front	¾"	19½"	24"	PB	1
D trough side (L)	¾"	17¼"	16"	PB	1
E trough side (R)	¾"	17¼"	16¾"	PB	1
F* front and back	1½"	5½"	27"	B	2
G* sides	1½"	5½"	21¾"	B	2
H cleats	¾"	1¼"	22½"	P	2
I cleats (sides)	¾"	1¼"	14¾"	P	2
J door	¾"	12⅝"	24"	PB	1
WORKTOP					
K* panel	1½"	22½"	34½"	LPB	1
L side banding	¾"	1½"	22½"	B	2
M banding	¾"	1½"	36"	B	2
VACUUM CONNECTOR AND SWITCH BLOCK					
N* connector	¾"	4" dia.		PB	2
O switch block	1½"	4"	4½"	B	1
FENCES AND GUARD					
P base	¾"	5"	7"	PW	2
Q supports	¾"	2"	7"	PW	2
R guides	¾"	2"	16½"	B	2
S sides	¾"	2⅛"	8¼"	B	2
T back	¾"	2⅛"	4¼"	B	1

*Initially cut parts marked with an * oversized. Trim them to finished size according to the how-to instructions.

Material Key: PB—particleboard, P—pine, LPB—laminated particleboard, B—birch, PW—plywood.

Supplies: #8X1" flathead wood screws, #8X1¼" flathead wood screws, #8X1¾" flathead wood screws, #8X2½" flathead wood screws, #10X½" flathead wood screws, ¾" drywall screws, 1¼" drywall screws, ¼X2" roundhead machine screws, 1⁄16" continuous hinge 24" long, panel adhesive, 90° street elbow (for 3" PVC pipe), 45° street elbow (for 3" PVC pipe), 3" PVC pipe 2' long, quick-set epoxy, 2 pieces of 25X37" plastic laminate, contact cement, four pieces of ¼" all-thread rod 4⅛" long, 4 knobs (Delta part no. 1087524, used on their miter gauge), ¼" wing nuts, ¼" flat washers, 14–¼" T-nuts, nylon pull (handle), 2 magnetic catches and plates, ¼X5X11¾" clear acrylic, 3½X3½" square corner hinge (Stanley part no. 741), ¼X20 carriage bolt 2" long, ¼" steel rod 2½" long, filler, sanding sealer, paint.

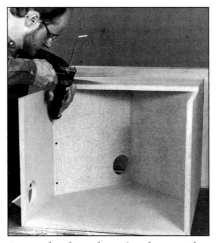

Screw the dust shoot in place, and caulk all joints for a tight seal.

(We chose birch stock; you also could use good-quality 2x6 material.) Bevel-rip a 1¼" chamfer along the top outside edge and a ¼" chamfer on the bottom outside edge of each piece. Miter-cut the pieces to length, and glue and clamp them to the bottom of the cabinet.

6. Glue and screw together the trough parts (D, E). Set the cabinet on its back, and slide the trough assembly into the cabinet so the top of the trough is 13" from the top of the cabinet where shown on the Section View drawing on *page 9.*

7. Drill mounting holes, and glue and screw the trough in position.

For near airtight joints, caulk all the seams between the trough parts and the cabinet as shown in the photo at *left.* (We used panel adhesive to caulk the joints.)

8. Cut the cleats (H, I) to size. Drill the mounting holes, and glue and screw the cleats in place.

9. Cut the door (J) to size. Cut a 1⁄16" continuous hinge to 24" long, and fasten it to the bottom of the door and then to the top edge of the front panel (C).

10. Cut a notch for the power cord below the front cleat (H) where shown on the drawing on the *opposite page.*

Next, add the worktop

1. Cut two pieces of ¾" particleboard to 23X35" for the worktop panel (K). Glue and clamp together the pieces with the edges flush. Trim all four edges of the panel for a 22½X34½" finished size.

2. From ¾" birch stock, cut the banding pieces (L, M) to length. Glue and clamp the banding pieces to the laminated panel (K). With a compass, mark a ¾" radius at each corner and cut to shape.

3. Cut two pieces of plastic laminate to 25X37". Using contact cement, adhere one of the plastic-laminate pieces to the top of the worktop. With a flush-trimming bit, rout the edges of the laminate *continued*

Cutting Diagram

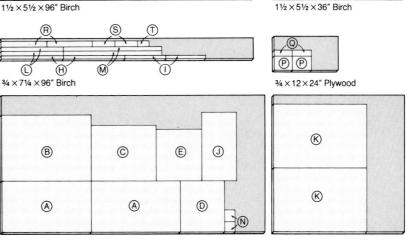

HEAVY-DUTY ROUTER TABLE
continued

flush with the outside edge of the worktop. Repeat the process with the bottom piece. Rout a ⅛" chamfer along the top and bottom of the worktop where shown on the Exploded View drawing.

4. To form the opening for the router plate, mark the centerpoints for four ¾" holes where shown on the Worktop Layout drawing at *right*. Bore the holes. Mark lines connecting the perimeters of the holes, and use a jigsaw to cut the opening to shape. Sand the opening smooth.

5. Rout a ⅜" rabbet ⅜" deep along the top inside edge of the opening. The top of the router plate should sit flush with the top of the worktop where shown on the Chamfer detail on *page 6*.

6. To provide additional clearance for installing and removing the router from the worktop, rout a 1" chamfer along the bottom of the opening where shown in the Chamfer detail on *page 6*. (To maneuver the Ryobi router through the opening, start by turning the height-adjustment knob to lower the router as far from the acrylic plate as possible. Then, you'll need to angle the router slightly and wiggle it through the worktop opening.)

7. Mark the location and cut the 3½"-diameter vacuum hole to size in the worktop.

Mount the worktop and rout the slot

1. Center and screw the worktop to the base where indicated on the Worktop Layout drawing *above right*.

2. Mark the miter-gauge slot location on the top of the worktop where dimensioned on the Worktop Layout drawing. As shown in the photo at *right,* clamp a board to the top of the worktop to act as a straightedge. Then, rout a slot to fit your miter gauge.

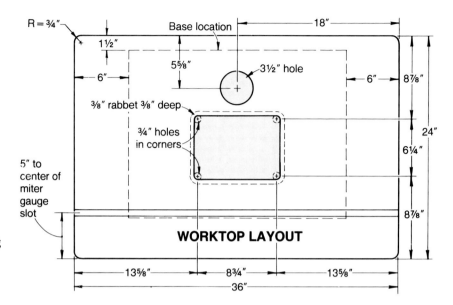

Rout a miter-gauge groove in the worktop.

Here's how to install the dust ports

1. Position the 90° street elbow PVC pipe in the hole from the bottom of the worktop where shown in the photo at *right*. Position the cabinet on its side. Using the Section View drawing *below right* for reference, drill two ⅛" pilot holes, and screw the 90° elbow in place.

2. Turn the cabinet upside down. Now, stick a 24" length of 3" PVC pipe through the top inlet hole and into the street elbow where shown in the photo. Mark the pipe length by wrapping tape around the pipe flush with the outside surface of the cabinet side. Remove the pipe.

3. With a hacksaw, trim the 3" PVC pipe to length, cutting at the tape line: Drill a pilot hole and fasten the straight piece of pipe to the 90° street elbow. Remove the tape.

4. Repeat the procedure above to attach the lower 45° street elbow and 3" PVC pipe.

Add the vacuum connectors and switch block

1. Cut two 4" squares from ¾" particleboard for the vacuum-hose connectors (N). Mark diagonal lines on each square to find center.

2. Measure the outside diameter of your vacuum hose (we measured ours at 2½" with an outside calipers). Using a compass, center and transfer the hole location to the connector blank. Mark a second circle ¾" on the outside of the first.

3. Drill a blade start hole and cut just inside the marked inner circle (the same diameter as your vacuum hose). Check the fit of the hose in the hole; it should fit snugly. Cut the outside circle to shape on the bandsaw and sand smooth.

4. Rout a ⅜" round-over along the top outside edge of each connector. Sand the connectors and glue and clamp each to the cabinet, centered over the previously cut holes.

5. Cut the switch block (O) to size. With #8✕2½" F.H. wood screws, glue and screw the block to the cabinet side (A) 6¾" from the front edge of the worktop.

continued

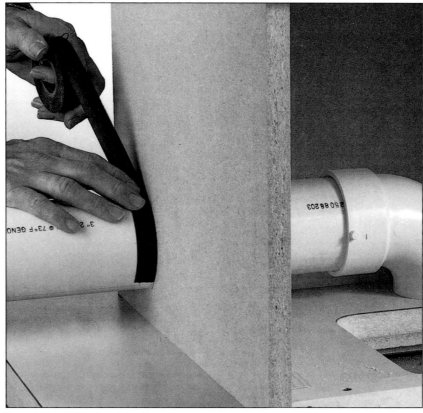

Insert the PVC pipe into the elbow, and mark the cutoff location with tape.

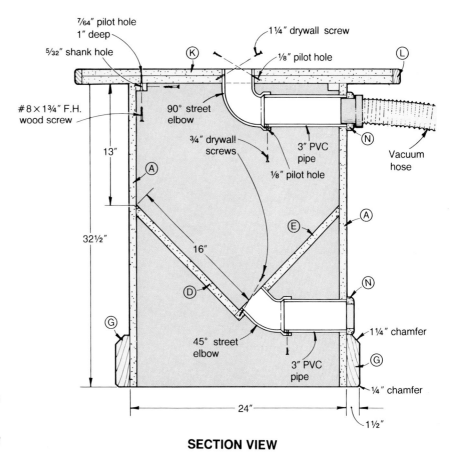

SECTION VIEW

HEAVY-DUTY ROUTER TABLE
continued

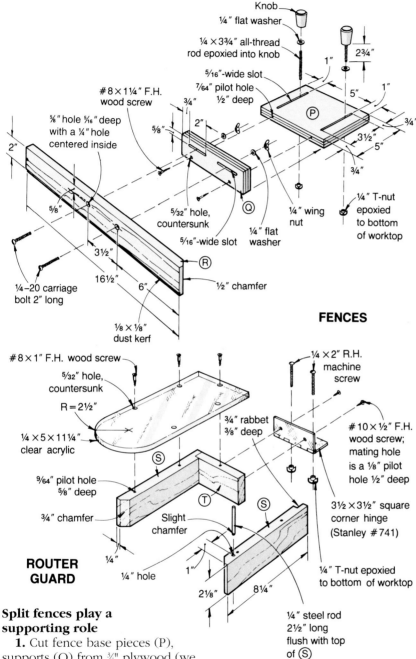

FENCES

**ROUTER
GUARD**

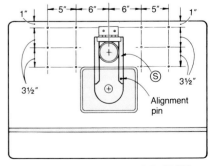

T-NUT AND GUARD LOCATION

5. With a hacksaw, cut four pieces of ¼" all-thread rod to 3¾" long. Epoxy and thread a knob onto one end of each threaded rod (see the Buying Guide for our source).

Guarding against eye injury

1. Cut the guard sides (S) and back (T) to size. Cut a ¾" chamfer along the front inside edge of each side piece where dimensioned on the Guard drawing *below left.* Cut or rout a ¾" rabbet ⅜" deep along the back inside edge of each side piece (S).

2. Glue and clamp the back piece between the side pieces. Attach the hinge to the back (T).

3. Position the router plate with attached router into the routed opening in the worktop.

4. Clamp the guard over the vacuum hole where shown on the T-Nut and Guard Location drawing *below.* Using the two outside hinge holes as guides, drill a pair of ¼" holes through the worktop.

5. With the guard clamped in place, drill a ¼" hole through the right-hand guard side (S) and through the router plate. Cut a piece of ¼" steel rod 2½" long. Grind or file a slight chamfer on the bottom end of the rod. Epoxy the rod into the hole in the guard side so ⅜" of the rod (the chamfered end) protrudes down into the hole in router plate. Do not epoxy the rod to the plate. The rod prevents the guard from moving when stock is pushed against the guard. Remove the guard from the worktop.

6. Cut the clear acrylic top to the shape shown on the Guard

Split fences play a supporting role

1. Cut fence base pieces (P), supports (Q) from ¾" plywood (we used birch plywood). Cut the guides (R) to size from birch stock. Cut a ⅛×⅛" dust kerf along the bottom front edge of each guide.

2. Mark the slot locations on the base and support pieces, using the Fences drawing *above, top,* for reference. Drill a 5⁄16" hole at each end of each marked slot. With a jigsaw or scrollsaw cut along the marked lines to form the slots.

3. Mark the centerpoints, and drill a pair of ¼" holes in each guide. Counterbore a ⅝" hole 5⁄16" deep centered over each ¼" hole on the front face of each guide.

4. With the bottom surfaces and ends of the supports (Q) and bases (P) flush, drill the holes, and glue and screw together each assembly. Check that Q is square to P.

drawing. (We used ¼" acrylic and cut it to shape with a bandsaw. See the Buying Guide for a source if you don't want to cut your own.)

7. At a speed of about 250 rpm, drill the mounting holes and screw the acrylic to the guard assembly.

Drill the holes and add the T-nuts

1. Remove the 90° elbow from the worktop, and remove the worktop from the cabinet. On the top of the worktop, mark the T-nut hole centerpoints where shown on the T-Nut Location drawing *opposite*. Check that the T-nut hole centerpoints align under the slots in the fence base parts (P). With a ¼" brad-point bit, drill 12 holes, backing the bottom with scrap to prevent chip-out. Switch to a ¹⁷⁄₆₄" bit, and enlarge the ¼" holes.

2. Countersink the holes on the top side. See the Chamfer detail accompanying the Exploded View drawing on *page 6* for reference.

3. Turn the worktop bottom side up. Counterbore ⁵⁄₁₆" holes ⅜" deep centered over each ¹⁷⁄₆₄" hole. See the Chamfer detail for specifics.

4. Insert a ¼" T-nut into each counterbore. Trace around the perimeter of each T-nut. With a spade bit, drill a ¾" hole ¼" deep where traced to house the T-nut head.

5. Being careful not to get any epoxy on the interior threaded portion, epoxy each T-nut in place

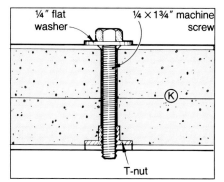

on the bottom side of the worktop. (Use the set-up shown *above* to position each T-nut squarely until the epoxy cures.)

How to apply a great-looking finish

1. Fill the voids and edges of the particleboard. (We used Durham's Rock Hard Putty.) Sand the cabinet, especially the edges, smooth.

2. Remove all the hardware, and mask the laminate top and bottom of the worktop. Next, apply a coat of lacquer sanding sealer to the cabinet, and guard.

3. Spray on a medium coat (no runs) of red gloss paint and allow it to dry until tacky. Then, spray on a thicker coat. The tacky coat provides a sticky surface for the follow-up coat. Repeat the procedure twice.

4. Finally, mask mating red areas, and paint the inside with an off-white, oil-based, semi-gloss enamel.

Final assembly before hitting the switch

1. Fasten the worktop to the cabinet. Install the PVC pipe fixtures.

2. Drill the holes, and attach the door pull. Next, fasten the strike plates to the back of the door and the magnetic catches to the front cleat (H). Attach the switch.

Buying Guide

• **Router plate.** ⅜x7¾x10¼" clear acrylic insert, radiused corners, and chamfered edges, catalog no. 102. If your router uses metric screws, specify router brand and model for a set of extra-long screws for mounting router to plate. For current prices, contact Woodhaven, 5323 West Kimberly Rd., Davenport, IA 52806, or call 800-344-6657 or 319-391-2386 to order.

• **Height-adjustment knob.** Knobs available for the Makita 3612, Bosch 1611 and 1611VS, Hitachi TR12, and Elu 3338. For current prices, contact Woodhaven, address above.

• **Hardware kit.** 4 knobs (similar to those shown) with ¼" threaded rod glued in place, 16–¼" T-nuts, nylon pull (handle), 2 magnetic catches and plates, ¼x4½x11¼" acrylic for guard. For current prices, contact Woodhaven, address above.

• **Power switch.** Catalog no. A526, For current prices, contact AMT, P.O. Box 70, Royersford, PA 19468, or call 215-948-0400 to order.

Project Tool List

Tablesaw
Portable jigsaw
Portable drill
Drill press
    Bits: ⁷⁄₆₄", ⅛", ⁹⁄₆₄", ⁵⁄₃₂", ¼", ¹⁷⁄₆₄", ⁵⁄₁₆", ¾"
Router
    Bits: ¼" and ¾" straight, chamfer, ⅜" rabbet, ⅜" round-over, flush trimming
Finishing sander

Note: We built the project using the tools listed. You may be able to substitute other tools or equipment for listed items you don't have. Additional common hand tools and clamps may be required to complete the project.

Something else to consider for your router table

Paul Pizzimenti says because the router cooling fan sucks up air from inside the table, the switch and speed-control dial cover might eventually fill with fine sawdust. He solved this problem by taping some loosely fitting clear 4-mil plastic over the controls where shown at *right*.

One additional change helps protect the router electronics and allows the router to breathe clean, cool air from outside the cabinet. Clamp a flexible 4" dryer vent hose around the top of the router

where shown and vent it through the cabinet side.

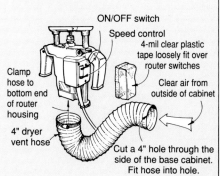

ON/OFF switch
Speed control
4-mil clear plastic tape loosely fit over router switches
Clamp hose to bottom end of router housing
Clear air from outside of cabinet
4" dryer vent hose
Cut a 4" hole through the side of the base cabinet. Fit hose into hole.

HOW YOUR CHOICE OF ROUTER BITS SHAPES UP

It happens before you know it—bit by bit, your router bit inventory builds until it's worth more than your router! A good, basic understanding of router bits and what they do can help you save some of that hard-earned cash and still get the most mileage from your router. With several hundred options, including prices from $5 to $100, facing you when you want to buy a router bit, it helps to narrow your choices. To do that, you have to know the types of bits and what they're intended to do. Starting with what bits are made of, we've organized the selection on these pages.

What router bits are made of

Stamped steel yields the least expensive router bits. Stamped into bit shape, rolled to configuration, then hardened, the flat steel used isn't meant for long-term routing or a depth of cut greater than ⅛" (it may bend). At about half the cost of a high-speed steel bit, it isn't practical to sharpen a stamped bit unless you do it yourself.

Climbing the price ladder to the under $10 range, you'll find *high-speed steel* (HSS) on the next rung. HSS bits, machined from solid-bar stock and ground to exact size, take the sharpest cutting edge of all bits. However, they dull quickly in very hard wood and composition materials. Dennis Huntsman of Porter-Cable suggests honing the flat side of a HSS bit with a sharpening stone for extra mileage.

Add an edge of tungsten carbide to HSS, double the price, and you have the even more expensive *carbide-tipped* router bit. Carbide-tipped bits stay sharper about 20 times longer than HSS or stamped

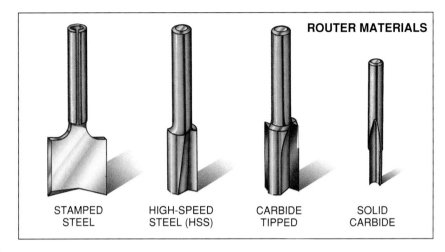

ROUTER MATERIALS

STAMPED STEEL   HIGH-SPEED STEEL (HSS)   CARBIDE TIPPED   SOLID CARBIDE

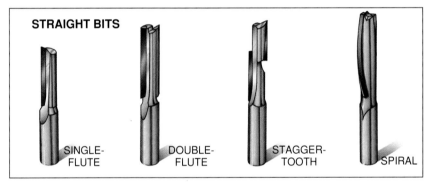

STRAIGHT BITS

SINGLE-FLUTE   DOUBLE-FLUTE   STAGGER-TOOTH   SPIRAL

steel. And they'll easily shear most woodworking materials except metal, which can cause them to fracture. A tiny fracture, advises the Robert Bosch Company's Don Duffy, makes investing in a new bit more sensible than resharpening. He notes that industrial-quality, carbide-tipped bits may be re-sharpened up to six times if they show no sign of chips or fracture. But remember that each time a bit has to be re-sharpened, its diameter will be reduced slightly.

Manufactured in short lengths (under 1"), *solid-carbide* bits are used primarily for trimming laminates. The short length helps prevent bit deflection and fracture.

Straight-cutting options

Straight bits cut a rectangular groove in the workpiece, plane an edge, or make a rabbet. In most applications they require a fence or other control device to guide their cut.

These bits have either one or two flutes, which provide wood-chip clearance. *Single-flute* bits, although actually making only half the number of cuts per revolution that *double-flute* bits do, cut faster because they have plenty of chip clearance.

Stagger-tooth straight bits, a two-flute type, have one cutter extending down from the top to slightly past center and the other coming up from the bottom the

Router bit vocabulary

Arbor: The part of the bit inserted into the router collet. On an assembled bit, the lower part of the arbor also holds the cutter and pilot tip. It may also be called the *shank*.

Assembled bit: A bit made up of several pieces. The arbor usually accommodates interchangeable cutters and pilot tips; also called an *interchangeable arbor*.

Carbide tip: A tungsten carbide alloy brazed to a router bit's cutting edge to increase bit life.

Cutting face: The cutting part of the bit, which can be either straight or angular (up-shear).

Flute: The opening in front of the cutting edge of a bit that provides clearance for the wood chips. Bits may have one or more flutes, and they may be straight, angular, or spiral. Flutes are also referred to as chip pockets or gullets.

Hook angle: The angle of the cutting face in reference to the center line of the bit. Hook angle affects feed rate and bit control.

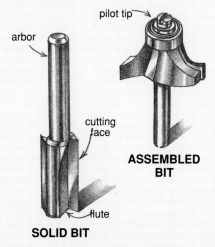

ASSEMBLED BIT

SOLID BIT

Pilot tip: The noncutting portion of a bit that limits the cut and guides the path of the bit by rubbing on the edge of the work. A pilot tip may be a ball bearing or a solid piece of steel.

Radial relief: The clearance angle behind the cutting edge on the periphery of the bit that keeps the bit from rubbing on the work.

Solid bit: A bit machined out of a single piece of tool steel. In some cases, a ball bearing pilot tip is fastened to it. Solid, or one-piece, bits usually have closer machining tolerance than assembled bits.

Stagger-tooth bit: A bit on which the cutting edges do not extend the complete length of the flute.

Up-shear: Another term for the inclined cutting face on a bit. The angle of the cutting face shears the chip in an upward fashion.

same distance. A stagger-tooth bit cuts as fast as a single flute, but leaves a smoother cut.

Another type of two-flute straight bit, the *spiral,* resembles a twist-drill bit, a feature that DML's Fred Garms says reduces chip accumulation and heat buildup. Due to its shearing action, the quality of the cut improves, but it cuts slower than other two-flute bits.

Edge-forming choices

Edge-forming bits cut on the edge of the work with the help of a pilot that controls their straight or irregular path. The pilot may be either integral or removable ball bearing. Bits in this category include rabbeting, cove, roundover, beading, camfer, and classical.

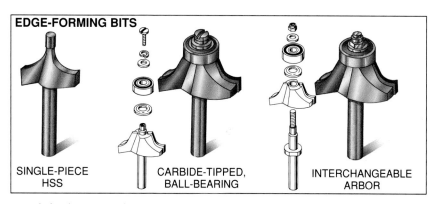

EDGE-FORMING BITS

SINGLE-PIECE HSS

CARBIDE-TIPPED, BALL-BEARING

INTERCHANGEABLE ARBOR

Solid-pilot or single-piece tips usually measure a ¼" or less in diameter, and because they rub on the edge of the work at the same rpm as the router, they can heat up and burn the wood. *Ball-bearing* pilot tips, on the other hand, roll along the edge at a slower rate than

the revolution of the bit. Because they turn only at feed rate, ball-bearing pilot tips won't burn your work unless the bearing jams due to accumulation of dirt or debris. Porter-Cable's Huntsman suggests buying an extra ball bearing when *continued*

HOW YOUR CHOICE OF ROUTER BITS SHAPES UP
continued

you purchase the bit so you won't have to interrupt a project in case a bearing fails. These bits come in diameters of ⅜" and larger.

Interchangeable-arbor or *assembled* bits can also fall into the edge-forming classification, although the cutter may be refitted and the pilot tip removed for groove-forming.

Groove-cutting selections

Requiring a guide or fence to direct their path, groove-forming bits are designed to cut a channel in the face of a workpiece, such as in sign-making. They are very similar to edge-cutting bits except that they have no pilot tip. In fact, groove-cutting bits may be used with a fence to rout an edge. Among the many choices in this group you'll find these often-used bits: round-nose (core box), ogee, classical, beading, dovetail, and veining.

Special-purpose alternates

Special-purpose bits actually fall into one or the other of the functional categories, but they deserve special notice because they fill highly specialized needs. Among the bits in this group are piloted and ball bearing groove-

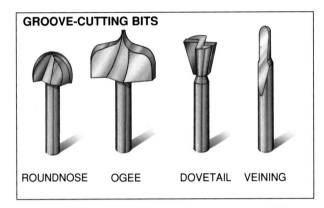

GROOVE-CUTTING BITS

ROUNDNOSE   OGEE   DOVETAIL   VEINING

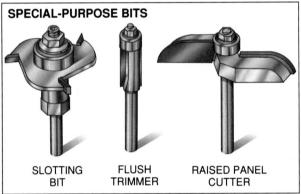

SPECIAL-PURPOSE BITS

SLOTTING   FLUSH   RAISED PANEL
BIT   TRIMMER   CUTTER

forming cutters called slotting bits, edge-forming bits such as the flush trimmer for plastic laminates, and molding-type bits such as the raised panel cutter. Many of these make repetitious production work easier.

HOW TO DODGE ROUTER BURNS

Exasperated readers often write and ask how they can avoid those nasty burns that occasionally pop up on routed surfaces. It's easy to understand their frustration. Burns such as the ones shown *below* can result in a sanding nightmare, or ruin the workpiece altogether. The truth is, you shouldn't have to deal with these burns at all. Just follow these simple measures.

1. Buy router bits with ball-bearing pilots

Although router bits with ball-bearing pilots cost a few dollars more, you'll find the extra investment worth it. Bearingless pilots heat up as they spin against the edge of a workpiece. Pilots with bearings run cooler because the tip of the router bit spins on the inside of the lubricated bearing, while the outside of the bearing coolly rolls along the workpiece.

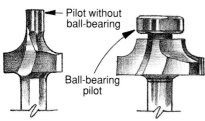

Pilot without ball-bearing

Ball-bearing pilot

2. Keep those bits sharp

Dull cutting edges—another source of friction—can burn a workpiece because they rub the wood instead of cleanly shearing it. The solutions: 1) Buy carbide-tipped bits—they stay sharp longer than steel bits and 2) Have your router bits sharpened at the first signs of dulling. Sharpening shops charge $4–$7 for bits less than 1" in diameter.

3. Take light, multiple cuts

Even a sharp, ball-bearing piloted router bit will burn wood if you feed the router too slowly or stop the machine while the bit is spinning. So, remember to keep the router moving at a steady rate (but not so fast that the router sounds labored). To accomplish this, take several light cuts as shown *below*, instead of one or two heavy ones that may cause you to slow the feed rate.

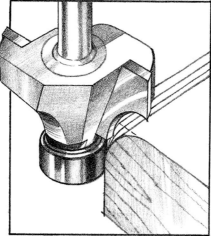

4. Don't get stalled on workpiece edges

Sometimes, it can be mighty difficult to start a router cut on the corner of a workpiece without easing the bit into the cut too slowly. To avoid burned corners, try to start the cut along an edge, then end the cut at the corner. If that's not possible, clamp a scrap block next to the starting corner as shown *above right*. The scrap must be the same thickness as the workpiece, and flush with its edge. This way, you can start the cut in the scrap and rout through the corner without slowing.

SCRAP   WORKPIECE

5. Use a router table whenever possible

A table-mounted router helps lessen your chances of accidental burning by giving you greater control over the workpiece, as well as feed rate. Because you don't have to worry about running out of cord, or balancing the router on the edge of a workpiece, you can concentrate on feeding the stock at a steady rate.

ROUTER STRAIGHTEDGE MAKES DADOES AND EDGE-JOINTING A SNAP

If you have ever put off building a project because it called for extra-long or tough-to-do dadoes, wait no more. Here comes our router straightedge to the rescue. You can make it in a few hours for under $15. And with it, you can just as easily rout one or a dozen dadoes, stopped or not. Plus, edge-jointing with your router also becomes a snap. So throw on your shop apron and safety glasses and let's head for the workshop!

Assembling the fence

Note: *The finished width of the base (A) will depend upon the size of the plastic subbase of your router and the size of straight bit used. As stated in the directions, we cut our base extra wide and then trimmed it to finished width later with a ¾" straight bit.*

1. From ½" plywood (we used 9-ply Baltic birch), rip and crosscut the base (A) and guide (B) to the sizes listed in the Bill of Materials *opposite.* Keep the front edge of

the guide perfectly straight, joint if necessary. When using later, the router slides along this edge and will transfer any imperfections to the workpiece.

2. Cut or rout a ⅛" rabbet ⅛" deep along one edge of the guide piece. When using, this rabbet acts as a sawdust notch.

3. To lay out the ³⁄₁₆" holes on the base, draw a line the length of the base 2" from what will be the back edge where shown in the drawing. Now, using a compass or dividers set at 2", step off and mark the hole locations on the base. Clamp a fence to your drill press and drill ³⁄₁₆" holes through the plywood base where marked. Back the piece with scrap to prevent chip-out.

4. Countersink *every* ³⁄₁₆" hole on the *bottom* side of the base to prevent the screwheads from scratching the piece being dadoed later.

5. Glue and clamp the guide piece to the base with the back edges and edges flush. Remove any glue squeeze-out from the sawdust notch before it dries. Sand the assembly smooth.

6. To trim the base to finished width, mount the straight bit you will use most often for routing dadoes (we used a ¾" bit) in your router. Clamp the base and guide assembly on the edge of your workbench, and rout ¼" into the plywood base (A). Check that the second cut won't hit your workbench, adjust the bit depth to cut all the way through, and finish routing through the base.

Making the stops

1. Cut a piece of the same ½" material used for the base and guide to 4×10". Using the Stop drawing *opposite* as a guide, lay out the stop (C) outline and slot location onto the blank where shown in the photo *below.* Repeat for the other stop.

2. Drill a ¼" hole at each end of each marked slot.

3. Fit a ¼" straight bit in your table-mounted router. Now, clamp a fence to the router table so the *center* of the straight bit is ½" from the inside edge of the fence.

4. Position the stop blank against the fence with the router bit protruding through one of the ¼" holes in the blank. Holding the blank firmly against the fence with one

hand, start the router with the other, and rout from hole to hole to form the slot as shown in the photo *opposite, bottom*. (In addition to using the ¼" holes as stop points, we also clamped a stop to the router table as shown in the photo.) Repeat this step to rout the slot in the second stop.

5. Cut or rout a ⅛" rabbet ⅛" deep along each end of the stop blank (see the Stop drawing for location) to act as sawdust notches. Cut the stops to shape from the blank with a bandsaw or scroll saw. Sand both pieces smooth.

6. Apply the finish to the stops, base, and guide. Applying a small amount of paraffin to the top surface of the base helps the router slide more easily. Attach the stops to the straightedge with ³⁄₁₆" flathead machine screws, washers, and wing nuts.

Putting the straightedge to work

Start by laying out the location of the dadoes or stopped dadoes needed on the workpiece, and set the straight bit to the needed depth. With the router turned off, position it on the base, check the position of the straight bit against the marked dado, and clamp the straightedge in position. If you plan on cutting dadoes with the same straight bit used in Step 6, position the front

edge of the base directly on the inside line marking the dado. If using a larger or smaller bit, you will need to adjust the position of the straightedge accordingly. Holding the router firmly against the guide, start the router, and move it into the wood and along the guide to cut the dado. Move the router in the direction noted by the arrow on the Exploded View drawing *below*.

For stopped dadoes, determine the length of the dado needed, position the stops, and tighten the wing nuts to hold the stops to the base. Position the straightedge on the workpiece and clamp it in position. Hold the router subbase against the guide but at a slight angle so the bit does not contact the piece to be routed. Start and lower the router to gently "plunge" the bit into the workpiece. Push the router from one stop to the other to rout the stopped dado. If available, a plunge router works great for stopped dadoes.

If you don't have a jointer and need to **edge-joint** irregular boards, remove the stops and clamp the front edge of the straightedge to the board being straightened so a minimum of ¹⁄₁₆" of the irregular edge protrudes the entire length of the board. Using a

straight bit, rout the irregular edge of the board straight.

Project Tool List
Tablesaw
Scrollsaw or bandsaw
Drill press
  Bits: ³⁄₁₆", ¼"
Router
  Bits: ⅛" rabbet, ¼" straight, ¾" straight
Finishing sander

Note: We built the project using the tools listed. You may be able to substitute other tools or equipment for listed items you don't have. Additional common hand tools and clamps may be required to complete the project.

Bill of Materials				
Part	Finished Size*			Mat.	Qty.
	T	W	L		
A* base	½"	4¾"	48"	P	1
B guide	½"	1½"	48"	P	1
C* stop	½"	4"	4"	P	2

* Parts marked with an * are cut larger initially; then trimmed to finished size. Please read the instructions before cutting.

Material Key: P—plywood
Supplies: 2–³⁄₁₆X1¾" flathead machine screws with flat washers and wing nuts, polyurethane, paraffin

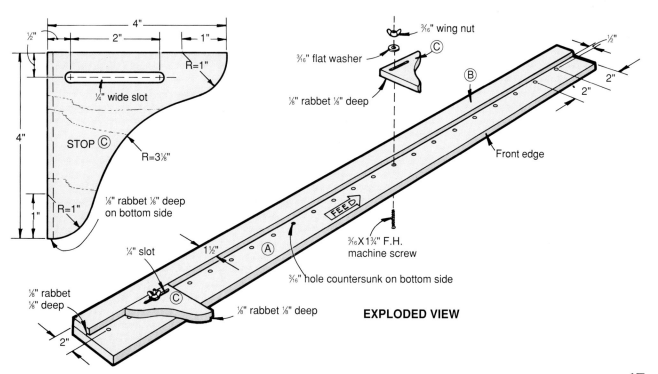

½"
4"
2"
1"
R=1"
¼" wide slot
STOP Ⓒ
R=3⅛"
4"
⅛" rabbet ⅛" deep on bottom side
R=1"
1"
¼" slot
⅛" rabbet ⅛" deep
2"
Ⓒ
³⁄₁₆" wing nut
³⁄₁₆" flat washer
Ⓒ
⅛" rabbet ⅛" deep
Ⓑ
½"
2"
2"
Front edge
1½"
Ⓐ
FEED
³⁄₁₆X1¾" F.H. machine screw
³⁄₁₆" hole countersunk on bottom side
⅛" rabbet ⅛" deep
EXPLODED VIEW

ROUTER TIPS AND TECHNIQUES

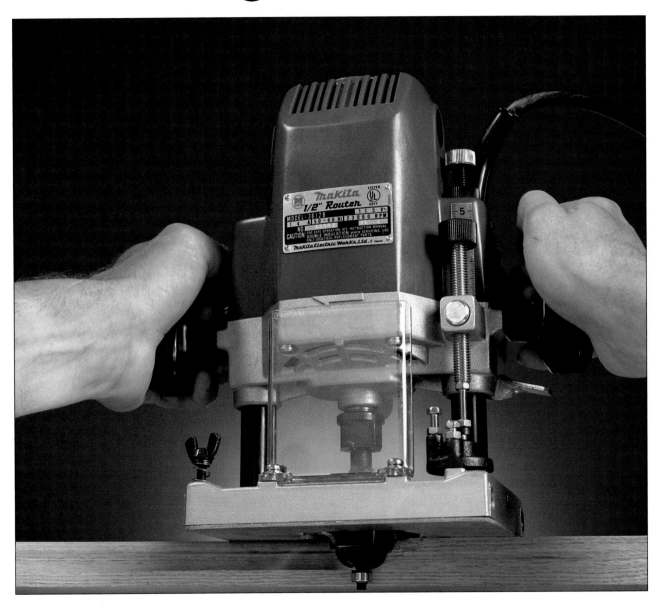

The information on these pages shows you how to get the most out of your router. You'll learn how to make mortise and tenon joints, use templates, create a variety of moldings, and fashion a tambour curtain.

ROUTER BASICS

Woodworkers love their routers, and it's easy to see why. Few tools can be put to more uses, and none rival the router's ability to quickly and gracefully enhance the appearance of a project. For best results when using your router, keep these tips in mind.

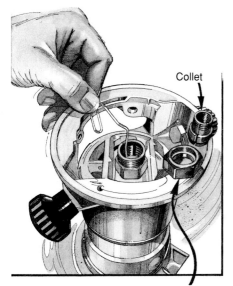

Collet

Collet locking nut

1. First, inspect the collet assembly for resin, wood dust, and other debris that can make bit removal difficult. To avoid sticky situations, start by removing the collet locking nut and collet. Then, blow away any loose debris. With a paper clip, gently scrape any gunk that remains as shown *above* (we removed the router subbase for clarity). Soften stubborn resins with lacquer thinner, then wipe clean.

Note: Always unplug the router when servicing the collet assembly or changing bits.

2. One other culprit can make bit removal a hassle: burrs, on the bit shank. Remove them with a few light file strokes as depicted

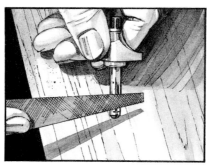

above. Now, securely lock the bit in the collet.

3. Before starting your router, always keep these safety pointers in mind:

• Wear eye and lung protection.
• Hold the router comfortably at arm's length and make sure you have enough available power cord to complete the job. If you run out of power cord, the bit will spin too long in one place and could burn the workpiece.
• Walk along with the router as you work, being careful not to overreach or lose your balance.

4. For the best possible cut, move the router along the edges of

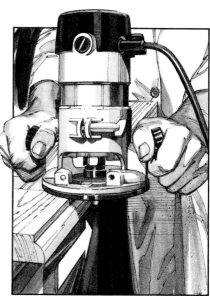

the surface in a counterclockwise direction as shown *above.* When routing all four edges, cut the end-grain edges first, then cut the edgegrain lengths to minimize edgegrain splinters.

Move the router at a consistent speed, and increase the feed rate if burning occurs. If the grain tears out, take several light passes.

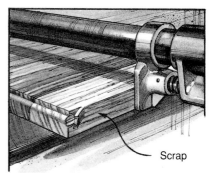

Scrap

5. When routing three edges of a surface, such as a shelf, back the final end-grain cut with scrap to prevent splintering of the workpiece. As shown *above,* the bit chipped out the scrap block, but left the corner of the workpiece crisp and clean.

FIVE GREAT ROUTER TRICKS

Actually, there's no slight of hand involved in working with a router—just a few tricks that help you charm more uses from it. For help with this article, we turned to three router wizards—Paul McClure of Denver, Brad Witt of Davenport, Iowa, and *WOOD*® magazine's very own Jim Downing—and asked them to conjure up their best feats of router magic. Although none of them could manage to levitate a router or make it disappear, they did pass along five of the niftiest tips ever to cross our workbench.

Template helps make quick, smooth circles

In his job as *WOOD*® magazine's design editor, Jim Downing uses draftsman's templates every day to draw circles in a fraction of the time required with a compass. So one day, Jim reasoned,"Why not design a template for routing circles in wood just as quickly?" A quick trip to the shop proved that Jim's idea made sense. In fact, he even figured out a system for cutting 28 different-sized circles from a template with only 7 holes.

To make a template for routing holes from 2⅝" to 6" in diameter, in ⅛" increments, first lay out the circles' centers where shown in the drawing *below* on a 15x23" piece of ¾" plywood. Since the size of the seven template holes must be exact, test each cut in scrap stock with a circle cutter before cutting the template holes. The photo at *right* shows cutting the holes in the template. To avoid chip-out on the back side of the template, cut the holes to about half of their depth, flip over the template, place the center bit into its hole, and complete the cut.

With all the holes cut, extend the four centerline marks down the walls of each hole with a try square. These marks help you center the template holes over the layout lines on your workpiece.

Now, mark the diameter of each template hole and save a copy of the chart *opposite*. This helpful chart shows what size straight router bit and guide bushing to use for each size hole.

In addition to cutting holes through stock, a router also will cut flat-bottom holes. When doing this, you may find that the base of your router doesn't span some of the larger template holes. When that happens, make a 12"-diameter auxiliary base of ¼" clear acrylic.

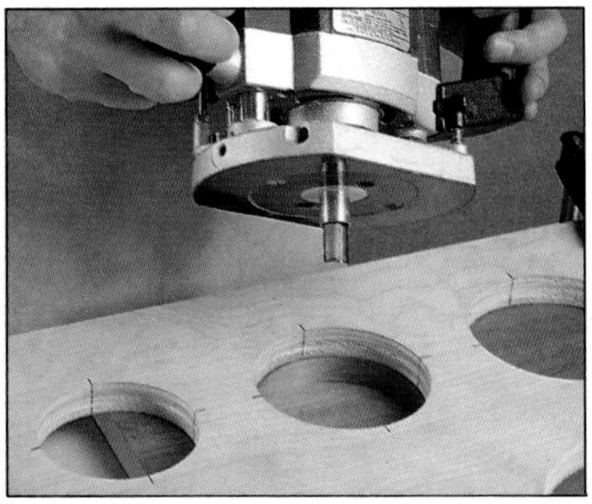

A circle template makes fast work of flat-bottom holes, such as the one *above*, as well as through-holes.

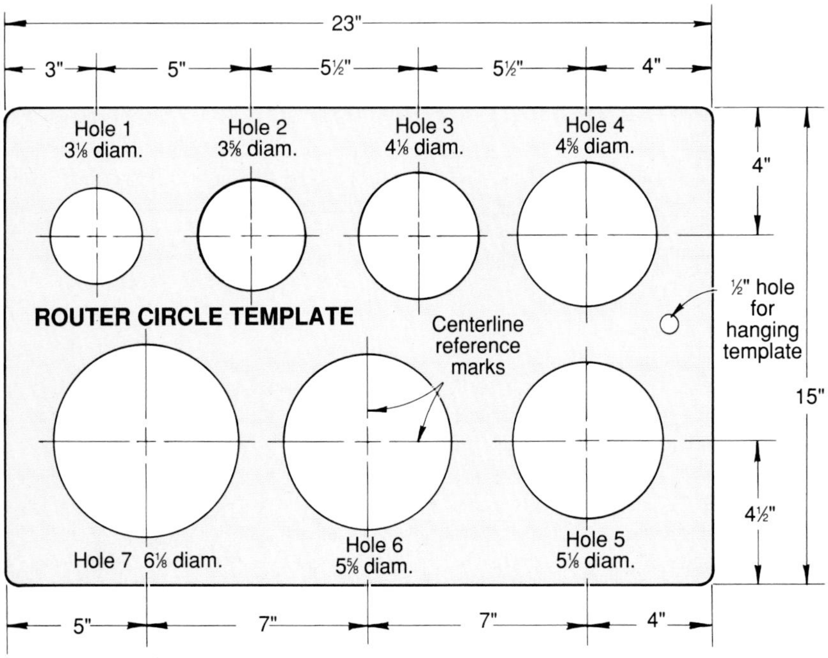
23"
3"
5"
5½"
5½"
4"
Hole 1
3⅛ diam.
Hole 2
3⅝ diam.
Hole 3
4⅛ diam.
Hole 4
4⅝ diam.
4"
ROUTER CIRCLE TEMPLATE
Centerline reference marks
½" hole for hanging template
15"
4½"
Hole 7 6⅛ diam.
Hole 6
5⅝ diam.
Hole 5
5⅛ diam.
5"
7"
7"
4"

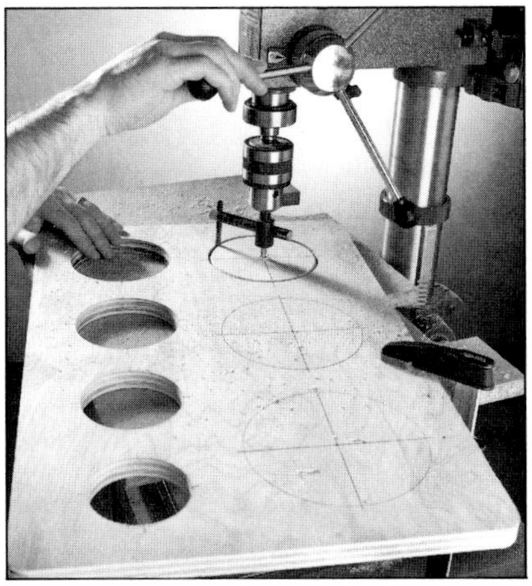

Cut the template holes with a 6" circle cutter. After cutting each hole to half its depth, flip over the stock and complete the cut to avoid chip-out.

Make 28 sizes of holes with one template

Desired hole size	Template hole	Guide brushing	Bit size
2⅝		¼	¼
2¾	Hole 1	⅝	¼
2⅞	3⅛" diam.	⅝	⅜
3		⅝	½
3⅛		¾	¼
3¼	Hole 2	⅝	¼
3⅜	3⅝" diam.	⅝	⅜
3½		⅝	½
3⅝		¼	¼
3¾	Hole 3	⅝	¼
3⅞	4⅛" diam.	⅝	⅜
4		⅝	½
4⅛		¾	¼
4¼	Hole 4	⅝	¼
4⅜	4⅝" diam.	⅝	⅜
4½		⅝	½
4⅝		¼	¼
4¾	Hole 5	⅝	¼
4⅞	5⅛" diam.	⅝	⅜
5		⅝	½
5⅛		¼	¼
5¼	Hole 6	⅝	¼
5⅜	5⅝" diam.	⅝	⅜
5½		½	½
5⅝		¼	¼
5¾	Hole 7	⅝	¼
5⅞	6⅛" diam.	⅝	⅜
6		⅝	½

Beautiful and functional louvers like these are just a router jig away.

Making louvers: it's a breeze

If you were to go into Jim Downing's home workshop, you'd see walls covered with jigs. And you would need to look only as far as his pet project to know why. While building a 30-foot sailboat in his garage, Jim has had to fashion one jig after another to help him construct its many wooden components. For instance, he found existing louvered-door construction techniques complicated and time-consuming. The solution? Another jig, of course.

As you can see from the photo *top right,* Jim's jig resulted in one lovely louver. To make a similar louvered insert, you'll need a plunge router and the jig we're operating at *right.* See the following pages for building instructions.

Stile stock

You can size the louver jig to accept any plunge router.

FIVE GREAT ROUTER TRICKS

continued

Bill of Materials

Part	Finished Size T	Finished Size W	Finished Size L	Mat.	Qty.
A	¾"	6½"	23"	P	1
B	¾"	1⅛"	3"	H	1
C	¾"	3"	5"	H	1
D	¾"	4"	4"	P	1
E	½"	*	**	H	2
F	½"	1"	**	H	2
G	½"	1"	2¼"	H	2

Material Key: P—plywood, H—any hardwood
*Width of router base +2"
**Length of router base +4¾"

It's a good idea to build the insert first, then make the frame. This way, you make minor adjustments in the size of the frame's opening to fit the insert—a simpler process than building a louvered insert to exact size. Follow these steps to make the insert's stiles and rails:

- Plan the number of louvers (each louver takes up 1" of the stile's length).
- Machine a piece of stock that's ⅞" thick, 2" wide, and to length (see the Laying Out Slot Spacing drawing at *right*). Then, lay out the spacing of the slots that hold the louvers.
- Clamp a piece of ⅞" scrap stock into the jig by placing the wood between the clamp block and router guide support. Secure the stock by tightening the handle. Now, set the jig's stops (G) for a 1 1/16"-long slot as shown *below*.
- With a straight bit, make an 11/16" deep test cut, lowering the bit in ⅛" passes.

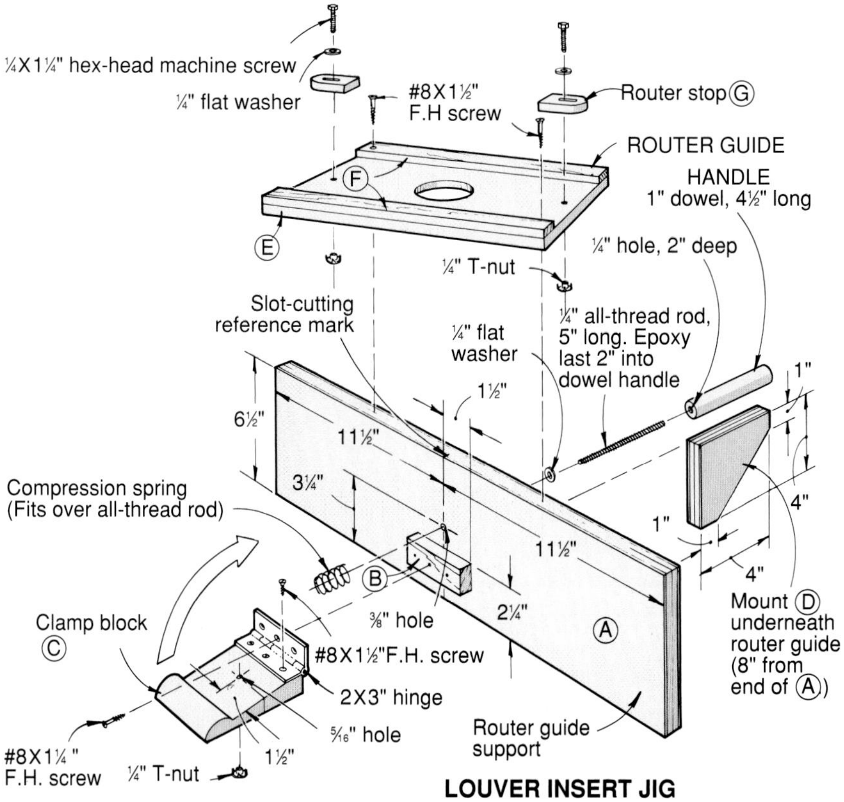
¼X1¼" hex-head machine screw
¼" flat washer
#8X1½" F.H screw
Router stop G
ROUTER GUIDE HANDLE 1" dowel, 4½" long
¼" hole, 2" deep
F
E
¼" T-nut
Slot-cutting reference mark
¼" flat washer
¼" all-thread rod, 5" long. Epoxy last 2" into dowel handle
1½"
1"
6½"
11½"
3¼"
Compression spring (Fits over all-thread rod)
4"
1"
11½"
4"
Mount D underneath router guide (8" from end of A)
B
⅜" hole
2¼"
A
Clamp block C
#8X1½"F.H. screw
2X3" hinge
5/16" hole
Router guide support
#8X1¼" F.H. screw
¼" T-nut
1½"

LOUVER INSERT JIG

LAYING OUT SLOT SPACING

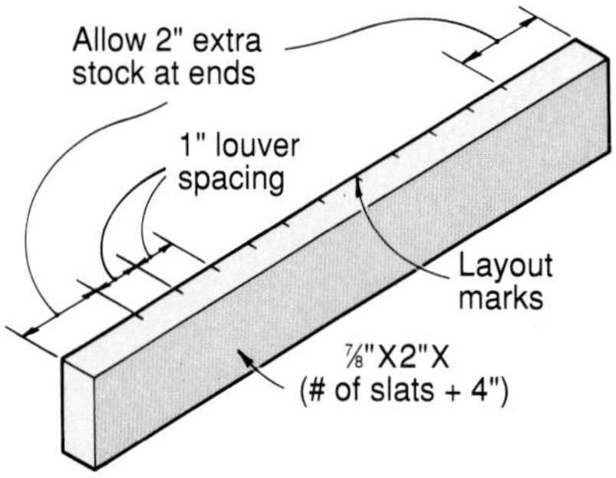
Allow 2" extra stock at ends
1" louver spacing
Layout marks
⅞"X2"X (# of slats + 4")

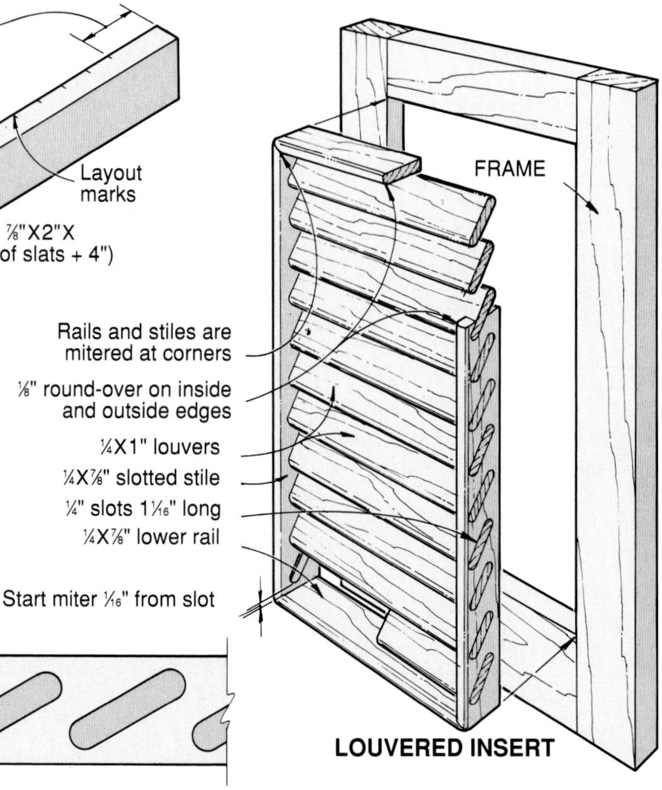
FRAME
Rails and stiles are mitered at corners
⅛" round-over on inside and outside edges
¼X1" louvers
¼X⅞" slotted stile
¼" slots 1 1/16" long
¼X⅞" lower rail
Start miter 1/16" from slot

LOUVERED INSERT

SETTING LENGTH OF SLOT

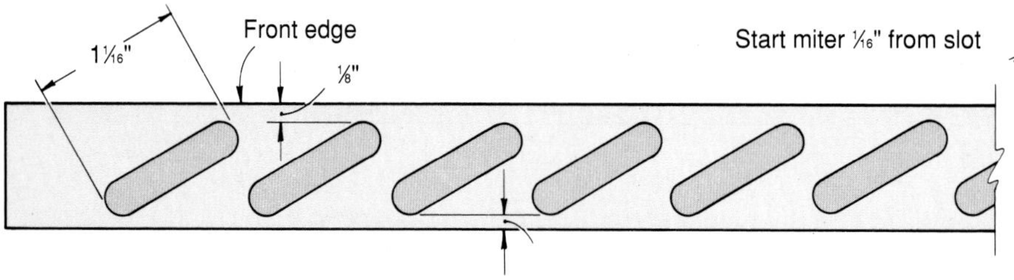
1 1/16"
Front edge
⅛"

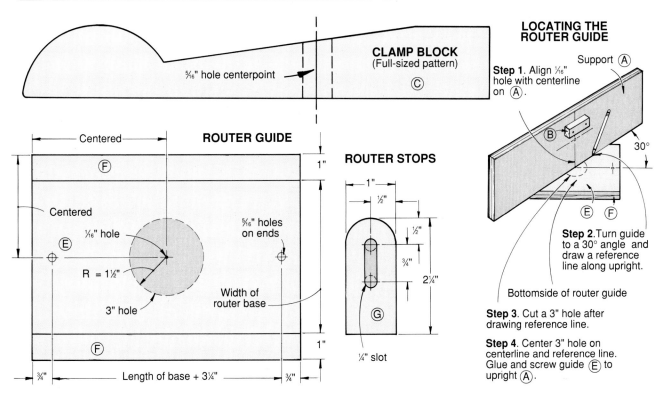

CLAMP BLOCK
(Full-sized pattern)
C

⁵⁄₁₆" hole centerpoint

LOCATING THE ROUTER GUIDE

Support A

Step 1. Align ¹⁄₁₆" hole with centerline on A.

B

30°

E F

Step 2.Turn guide to a 30° angle and draw a reference line along upright.

Bottomside of router guide

Step 3. Cut a 3" hole after drawing reference line.

Step 4. Center 3" hole on centerline and reference line. Glue and screw guide E to upright A.

ROUTER GUIDE

Centered

F

1"

Centered

¹⁄₁₆" hole

E

⁵⁄₁₆" holes on ends

R = 1½"

3" hole

Width of router base

F

1"

¾"   Length of base + 3¼"   ¾"

ROUTER STOPS

1"
½"
½"
¾"
2¼"

G

¼" slot

Rip both stiles from one workpiece, then rip the rails.

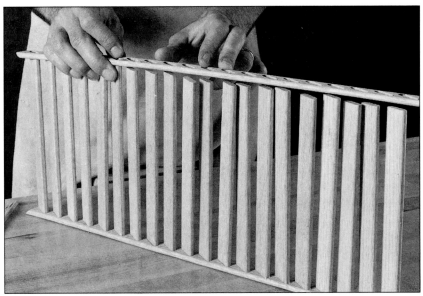

Use a gentle hand to attach the stiles to the louvers. To avoid splitting the stiles, remachine any louvers that don't fit.

• When satisfied with your test cuts, clamp the stile stock into the jig, aligning the first louver mark with the jig's reference mark. Cut a slot at each louver mark.

• With the slot-side of the stock facing the fence, rip the stock into two ¼"-thick stiles as shown *above*.

• From the leftover stock, rip the ¼"-thick rails.

• With a ⅛" round-over bit, shape the inside and outside front edges of the rails and stiles. Leave the back edges square.

• Miter the rails and stiles (start the stile miters ¹⁄₁₆" from the top and bottom slots).

To make the louvers, first rip a ¼"-thick test strip from a piece of 1"-thick stock. Round over all four edges of the strip with a ⅛" rounding-over bit and check its fit into the louver slots. Adjust your

tablesaw and router until the test strip fits in the slots. Now, cut the louver stock to lengths ¹⁄₁₆" shorter than the rails and assemble the louvers and stiles as shown *above*. Be patient as you insert the louvers into the stiles—the stiles may split if you try to force a too-large louver into them. Glue the rails in place.

continued

FIVE GREAT ROUTER TRICKS
continued

Biscuit joinery with a router? You bet!

Brad Witt built his first router table when he was 12, and in the 24 years since then, he's parlayed his router expertise into a full-time router-accessories business. So naturally, as plate joiners (sometimes called biscuit joiners) grew in popularity among home woodworkers during the past five years, Witt explored ways that a router could do the same job. His answer: Use a slotting cutter in a table-mounted router to cut a hole that accepts the football-shaped wooden biscuits. That was the easy part.

Since standard plate-joiner biscuits don't fit the slotting-cutter hole, the hard part was fashioning some biscuits that would fit into this slot. Now, Witt markets a biscuit (see the Buying Guide at *far right*) that not only fits, but also has a clear advantage over standard 1¾"- to 2⅜"-long biscuits. With a

A router table can handle many of a plate joiner's jobs.

length of only 1¼", you can use Woodhaven's biscuits on 1½"-wide face frame members. The pressed-wood biscuits will slide easily into a ¼" slot, then expand when glued to form a solid joint.

Here's how Brad's system works: First, build the fence shown *below* and obtain a 1½"-diameter, ¼" slotting cutter with a ½" pilot bearing (see Buying Guide at *right*). Then, dry-clamp your frame together, and mark the centers of the joints as shown at *left*. Now, center the fence on the router table by raising the slotting-cutter's pilot through the hole

in the fence's acrylic guard. Clamp the fence in place. Line up the biscuit center mark of your workpiece with the scribed centerline on the fence guard, and clamp a square scrap board to the table to guide the work-piece into the cutter as pictured *above*. After cutting the slots, apply glue to all the joint edges, and assemble the frame pieces.

Buying Guide
• **Biscuits, splines, and slotting cutter.** For current prices, contact Woodhaven, 5323 W. Kimberly Rd., Davenport, IA 52806. Phone: 800-344-6657.

Biscuit center mark

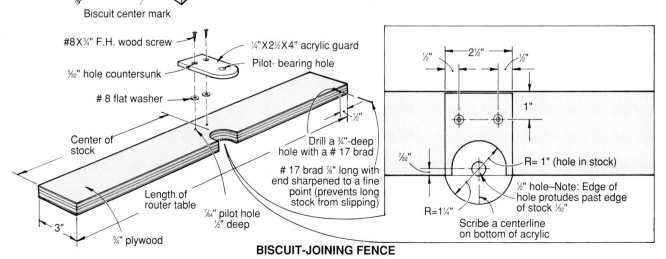

BISCUIT-JOINING FENCE

#8 X ¾" F.H. wood screw
¼" X 2½ X 4" acrylic guard
Pilot- bearing hole
5⁄32" hole countersunk
8 flat washer
Center of stock
Length of router table
7⁄64" pilot hole ½" deep
3"
¾" plywood
Drill a ¾"-deep hole with a # 17 brad
17 brad ⅞" long with end sharpened to a fine point (prevents long stock from slipping)
½"
½"
2½"
½"
1"
7⁄32"
R= 1" (hole in stock)
½" hole–Note: Edge of hole protudes past edge of stock 1⁄32"
R=1¼"
Scribe a centerline on bottom of acrylic

Make super-simple frames with a ⅜" rabbeting bit

Our good buddy Paul McClure, a crackerjack wood technologist, has done nearly everything in woodworking—he's been an instructor, exotic hardwood buyer, and retail woodworking store owner. So it didn't surprise us when this regular contributor to *WOOD*® magazine came up with a slick way of making door frames. His technique uses ¾"-thick stock and calls for ⅜" rabbeted edges to help form strong joints between the rails and stiles. The rabbet accommodates a plywood panel or ⅛" glass with ¼" stops as shown at *top right*.

First, set a ⅜" rabbeting bit for a ⅜"-deep cut. To test this, cut a few scrap blocks from the frame stock, and adjust the bit's depth until it removes exactly one-half of the thickness of the stock. We routed the scraps shown at *middle right* to demonstrate some test results.

Now, refer to the drawing *below right* as a guide and cut the stiles to length and the rails to the width of the frame opening plus ¾" to allow for the two ⅜" rabbets. Rout a rabbet along one of the long edges on the backside of each piece. Then, flip over the rails and clamp them to your workbench as we're doing above. Before rabbeting each end of both rails, you must align the ends of the rails flush with the scrap blocks so the bit's pilot has a straight surface to ride on. This arrangement prevents the router from tearing out the corners of the workpieces or rounding them off.

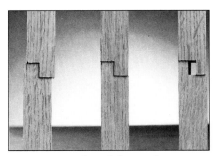

A router provides you an easy way to make attractive frames with smooth, clean rabbets.

Our tests produced from *above*, a too-shallow cut, a correct cut with flush faces, and a too-deep cut.

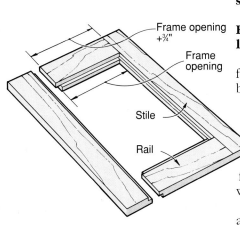

Scrap blocks

Scrap blocks (one with a rabbet) provide a straight, continuous surface for the bit's pilot to ride on.

Flush-trimming jig saves you loads of time

We've seen plenty of other jigs for trimming solid-wood edge bandings flush with a plywood surface, but none of them met our requirements for versatility or ease of use. So, ever-resourceful Jim Downing devised the jig *above right* that not only trims flush along straight edges, but also works its way into corners.

Once you build the jig and attach your router to it, insert a ½"

hinge-mortising bit and adjust it so it's just a hair *above* the plywood surface. Keep a steady hand on both the wooden knob and router handle to give a flat surface.

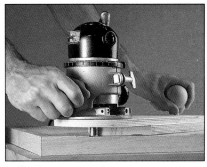

A flush-trimming jig saves you hours of planning and scraping.

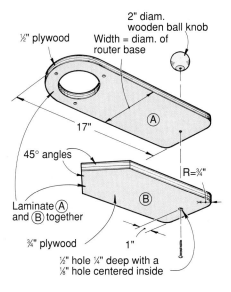

½" plywood

2" diam. wooden ball knob
Width = diam. of router base

17"

Ⓐ

45° angles

Laminate Ⓐ and Ⓑ together

R=¾"

Ⓑ

¾" plywood   1"

½" hole ¼" deep with a ⅛" hole centered inside

TOP VIEW

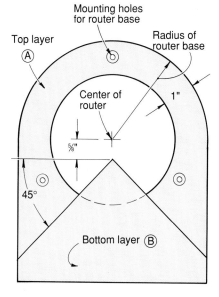

Mounting holes for router base

Top layer Ⓐ

Radius of router base

Center of router

1"

⅝"

45°

Bottom layer Ⓑ

Frame opening +¾"

Frame opening

Stile

Rail

BASIC MORTISE AND TENON JOINERY

Our mortising jig and a plunge router make the going easier and more accurate than ever before.

For some reason, the words "mortise and tenon" scare lots of woodworkers. Many hobbyists assume that only true craftsmen have the skills necessary to master this superstrong joint. Not so! Anyone willing to invest the time it takes to read this article, and make the mortising jig we have developed, can fashion good-looking, tight-fitting joints the first time out.

While many variations of the mortise and tenon exist, getting into all of them at the outset will only confuse you. That's why we decided to concentrate on the basics. We'll use a simple frame with hidden mortise and tenon joints as the example, but the information we present applies to other situations as well.

Before reading on, you may find it helpful to study the sketch *below.* It will familiarize you with the terminology we'll be using later on. It also gives you some standard sizing information for mortises and tenons.

Note: *If you want to know how to lay out mortise and tenon joints for raised panel doors or for joining the legs and aprons of tables (or the legs and rails of chairs), see* page 31.

Cutting the frame members to size

After determining the finished size of the frame you want to construct, cut the stiles and rails to size. Don't forget to factor the length of the tenons into the length of the rails. Cut an extra rail, too—it will serve as a layout template.

Laying out the mortises and tenons

You'll be handling the various frame members a lot during and after layout. So, to avoid confusion (not to mention cutting errors), start by carefully laying them out, faceup, as they will be when assembled. Then, number each joint with a pencil, identify the outside edge of each member, and mark the inside edge of each rail on both ends of each stile, as shown *opposite, top.*

Now, make yourself a layout template, using the extra rail you cut earlier. First lay out any rabbets, grooves, or profiles you plan to cut into the frame members. Then, using a square, mark the length of the tenons on the template as shown *opposite, top center.* Remember that the length of hidden tenons typically equals ⅔ the width of the mortised frame members.

Next, with a marking gauge, lay out all four of the tenon's borders on the template where shown in the sketch *opposite, top right.* You may want to refer to the anatomy drawing *below,* and review the standards presented there.

Once you've marked the template, use it and the marking gauge to transfer all of the lines from the template onto the frame members. The series of sketches *opposite, bottom,* shows you the progression we use to do the layout work. Note that once we set the marking gauge each step of the way, we mark both the mortise and tenon on all of the rails and stiles before changing the setting. Doing this ensures that the mortises and tenons will be mirror images of each other. Note also that we set the gauge from the face side of the template for both lines that define the thickness of the tenons. This is just in case the members vary slightly in thickness.

continued

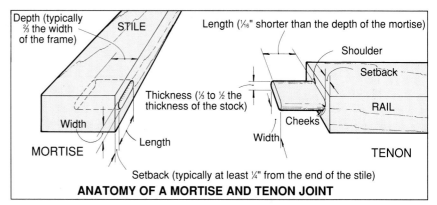

ANATOMY OF A MORTISE AND TENON JOINT

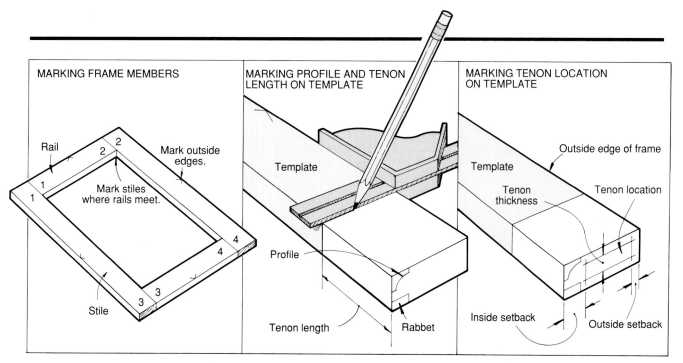

MARKING FRAME MEMBERS

Rail

Mark outside edges.

Mark stiles where rails meet.

Stile

MARKING PROFILE AND TENON LENGTH ON TEMPLATE

Template

Profile

Tenon length

Rabbet

MARKING TENON LOCATION ON TEMPLATE

Template

Outside edge of frame

Tenon thickness

Tenon location

Inside setback

Outside setback

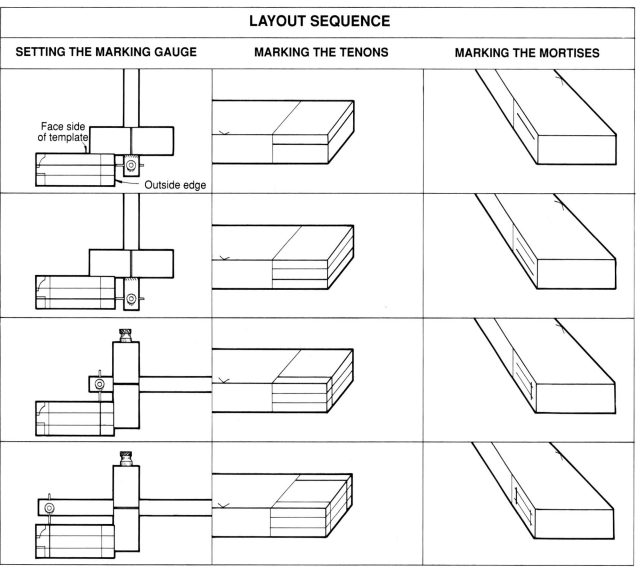

LAYOUT SEQUENCE

SETTING THE MARKING GAUGE	MARKING THE TENONS	MARKING THE MORTISES

Face side of template

Outside edge

BASIC MORTISE AND TENON JOINERY

continued

Our mortising jig: it does the job quickly and accurately

As you probably know, there are several ways to cut mortises, both by hand and with machines. Cutting mortises by hand has always seemed too labor-intensive to us, especially if we have lots of them to make. And while you can purchase a mortising attachment for your drill press, if you have one, we think our jig is faster and more accurate.

The Exploded View drawing and the detail drawings that accompany it *(opposite page)* give you the information you need to build the jig. And on *this page* we show you how to set it up and use it.

Note: The jig does require that you have a plunge router to make the cuts. If you don't have one already, we think the money you spend on this versatile tool will be well worth it. It not only makes cutting mortises a snap, you can also put it to good use for cutting stopped dadoes and grooves, template routing, and many other cutting chores. Several router manufacturers have one or more plunge models in their line. Also, you'll need a long-shanked, carbide-tipped straight router bit.

Buying Guide

• **Quick-release toggle clamp.** Catalog no. 173-003. For current prices, contact Woodworker's Supply, 1108 North Glenn Rd., Casper, WY 82601. 800-645-9292.

• **Stop collars.** ½" set collars. Stock no. S/C ½. For current prices, contact Standard Bearings, PO Box 823, Des Moines, IA 50304. 515-265-5261.

Cutting the mortises

1. Start by securing the jig in a vise. Then, fit one of the stiles in the jig, and position and clamp the fence so that the stile fits snugly against the alignment blocks.

Note: Always check to be sure that the face side of the piece being mortised is against the jig. Doing this ensures that the face side of frame members will be flush with each other.

2. Slide one end of the stile toward the center of the jig, and clamp it there with the hold-down clamp. Now, loosen the wing nuts holding the router base in place, and carefully center the router bit over

the mortise. Retighten the wing nuts. Don't worry too much about the router base being exactly perpendicular to the jig; it needn't be.

3. To limit the travel of the router, line up the bit with each end of the mortise and set the stop collars with an allen wrench.

4. To ensure consistent placement of succeeding mortises, clamp a stop block to the jig. Be sure to snug the block up against the end of the material.

5. When setting the depth of cut, keep in mind that you want the mortise to be approximately ⅟₁₆" deeper than the length of the tenon. This extra depth forms a reservoir for glue that will be forced to the bottom of the mortise during glue-up. If you don't provide space for the glue to build up, even with heavy clamp pressure you may not be able to bring the stiles and rails completely together to form a tight joint.

6. It's best to make several shallow passes with the router when cutting the mortises. We generally move down in ¼" increments. When you've reached the bottom, make

continued

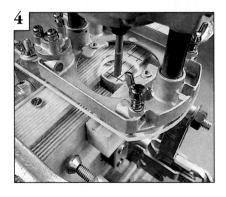

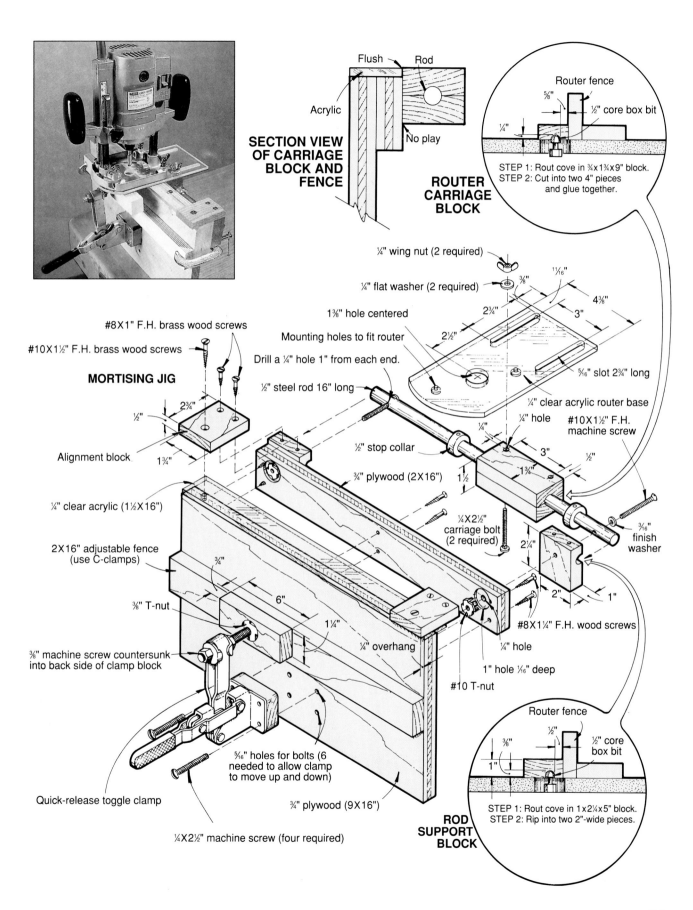

SECTION VIEW OF CARRIAGE BLOCK AND FENCE

Flush
Rod
Acrylic
No play

ROUTER CARRIAGE BLOCK

Router fence
⅝"
½" core box bit
¼"

STEP 1: Rout cove in ¾ x 1¾ x 9" block.
STEP 2: Cut into two 4" pieces and glue together.

¼" wing nut (2 required)
¼" flat washer (2 required)
1⅜" hole centered
Mounting holes to fit router
Drill a ¼" hole 1" from each end.
½" steel rod 16" long

⅜"
11/16"
2¾"
4⅜"
2½"
3"
5/16" slot 2¾" long
¼" clear acrylic router base

#8X1" F.H. brass wood screws
#10X1½" F.H. brass wood screws

MORTISING JIG

Alignment block
½"
2¾"
1¾"

½" stop collar
¾" plywood (2X16")
1½
¼"
¼"
3"
½"
1¾"
¼" hole
#10X1½" F.H. machine screw

3/16" finish washer

¼" clear acrylic (1½X16")

2X16" adjustable fence (use C-clamps)

⅜" T-nut

¾"
6"
1¼"
¾"
¼" overhang

¼X2½" carriage bolt (2 required)
2¼"
2"
1"

⅜" machine screw countersunk into back side of clamp block

#8X1¼" F.H. wood screws
¼" hole
1" hole 1/16" deep
#10 T-nut

Quick-release toggle clamp

5/16" holes for bolts (6 needed to allow clamp to move up and down)

¾" plywood (9X16")

¼X2½" machine screw (four required)

ROD SUPPORT BLOCK

Router fence
⅜"
½"
1"
½" core box bit

STEP 1: Rout cove in 1 x 2¼ x 5" block.
STEP 2: Rip into two 2"-wide pieces.

BASIC MORTISE AND TENON JOINERY
continued

another plunge at both ends of the mortise to remove any minor irregularities that may be left from previous cuts. When you're finished with the first mortise, remove the stile and insert the other one, again making absolutely sure that the face side rests against the jig.

7. To cut the mortises at the other end of the stiles, you need to move the stop block to the other side of the router bit. To position it correctly, first slide the router to the right until it makes contact with the stop collar. Then, insert one of the stiles into the jig, face side in, carefully aligning the router bit with the right-hand end of the mortise, and clamp the stock in place. Now, clamp the stop block against the end of the stile, and cut the remaining mortises as before.

Cutting the tenons

1. Place one of the stiles face side down, on your table saw, and set the height of the blade, using the mortise as a guide.

2. Now, using your layout template, set the rip fence to

control the tenon length. To ensure that the template is perpendicular to the rip fence, hold the template against the miter gauge.

3. To test the blade height setting, position your layout template, facedown, on the table saw, and make one pass at the end of it. Then check it against one of the mortises as shown. Make any necessary adjustments.

4. Remove the material from the *face side* of each end of each rail. You will notice some saw marks left by the dado blade, but don't worry about them. The tenons needn't be smooth.

5. Again using your template, this time with the *back side facing down,* cut away a portion of the material from its back side. Now, check the fit of the tenon in one of the mortises. You want a snug, but not a tight, fit. Raise or lower the blade to adjust the thickness of the tenon, if necessary, then remove the material from the back side of each end of each rail.

6. To remove the material from the outside and inside setback portions of the tenons, turn once again to your trusty template, elevate the blade to the proper height for each setback, make test cuts on your template, check them against the mortise, and remove the remaining material.

7. To round off the corners of each of the tenons, we use a sanding belt wrapped around a piece of plywood. With it, we chamfer each corner and round it over slightly. Take care not to sand the top and bottom cheeks of the tenons, though. By doing so, you can cause distortion of the frame members. Also be sure to hold the sanding block square to the tenon. Accidentally beveling the tenons will weaken the mechanical strength of the joint.

8. After rounding the corners, you'll still need to remove some material at the base of the tenons.

Otherwise, you'll find that the joints won't close all the way. We use a chisel to remove the excess material.

Gluing and clamping the frame

If you've made all of your cuts carefully, this part of the project should be a piece of cake. It's a good idea to dry-clamp the frame to make sure that the members fit together tightly and that the face sides of the frame members are flush.

If everything checks out, apply glue to both the tenons and the mortises, assemble the frame, and clamp until the glue sets up. Be sure to check the frame for square while the glue is still wet.

Two variations on the mortise and tenon theme

Raised-panel door and table and chair joints each call for a slightly different layout strategy.

The haunched mortise and tenon

When building raised-panel doors, it's common practice among woodworkers to cut a groove along the inside edge of each frame member to accept the panel. When faced with this situation, you need to create a haunch, or lip, on the tenon to fill the void created by the groove.

To do this, start by laying out the borders of the tenon as explained on *page 27*. Then, measure the depth of the groove in the frame, and lay out the haunch where shown in the detail drawing *above right*. Remember that the length of the haunch equals the depth of the groove. Cut away the material only back to this line, and you will have created the haunch you need.

The mortise and tenon with reveal

Lots of experienced woodworkers favor the mortise and tenon joint when joining the legs and aprons of tables (and for the legs and rails of chairs) because of its great strength. When laying out the location of the mortises on the legs you must first decide how much of a reveal (or setback) suits you. Aprons typically set back about ⅛" from the outside edge of the legs.

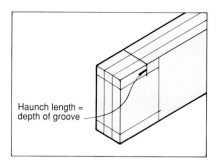

Haunch length = depth of groove

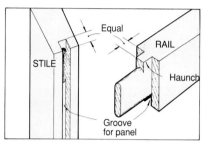

Equal
STILE
RAIL
Haunch
Groove for panel

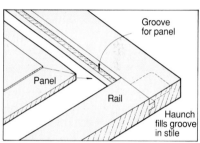

Groove for panel
Panel
Rail
Haunch fills groove in stile

Then, in the case of a table, lay out the legs and aprons as shown in the detail *below*, number each of the joints for easy identification, carefully mark the outline of the aprons on the legs, and lay out the mortises and tenons as instructed on *page 27*.

When laying out a leg/rail joint for a chair, you follow pretty much the same procedures. However, you will have to clamp the legs and rails together when marking the outline of the rails on the legs.

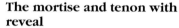

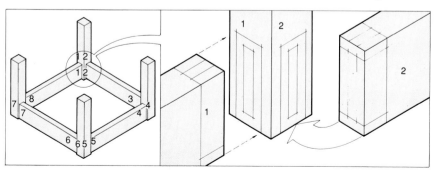

TEMPLATE ROUTING

Production woodworkers swear by them. And so do craftspeople who sell their work at crafts fairs, church bazaars, and shopping malls. But to most other woodworkers, templates remain somewhat of a mystery.

Why do people who depend on woodworking for their livelihood think so highly of templates? Two reasons, actually. First, they know that a correctly made template enables them to make more accurate cuts than would otherwise be possible. And second, with templates, these pros can work quickly without fear of making costly mistakes.

Granted, as a home woodworker you may not be overly concerned with speed. But if you're like us, you will appreciate the accuracy you can achieve with them.

Once you master the basics of making templates, you'll be able to do all sorts of projects you never thought possible. Say, for example, you want to make a carving board with a decorative pattern carved into it. No problem! You can make one—or a hundred if you want—with a template. And what about signs with your name incised into them? You can do those, too, and they'll turn out great.

Sound like fun? We think you'll find the techniques we cover on these next several pages as intriguing as we did—and just as helpful. Developing these certainly opened our eyes to many new woodworking possibilities, and we're sure that reading it will do the same for you.

What is template routing, anyway?

Think of a template as a rigid pattern that defines the shape of the design you are cutting into your project. But a template does more than that. It also controls the

cutting action of the router. It just won't allow the router to make a mistake.

We will be telling you about two different techniques here—*template guide routing* and *pin routing* with our Delta-Wing Pin Routing Attachment. Though similar, they differ in several key respects. As you can see by looking at the two cutaway sketches *below* and *opposite*, when template guide routing, the router cuts from above the work. Not so when pin routing with our attachment! Here, a guide pin follows the pattern in the template. You don't even see the cutting action when pin routing.

Also, with template guide routing, the template opening must be slightly larger than the size of the cutouts to be routed. Pin routing templates, on the other hand, duplicate the size of the pattern exactly.

There's one final difference to notice as well. If you use a template guide to make your project, the template itself needs to be somewhat larger than the work to accommodate the *positioning blocks* that hold the work in place.

With pin router projects, you tack the template to a *carrier* and hold it in place over the work with *double-faced tape* and *positioning*

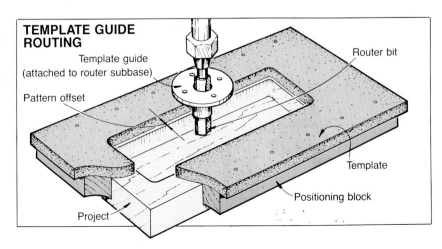

TEMPLATE GUIDE ROUTING

Template guide (attached to router subbase)

Pattern offset

Router bit

Template

Positioning block

Project

*blocks.*With this technique, the template and the work piece are identical in size.

Each technique has advantages in certain situations. Use these guidelines to determine which technique to use:

• Template guide routing works well with simpler projects of *any size.* Many people rout the mortises for door hinges and make recessed cuts in lettered signs with template guides.

• Use the pin routing technique when you're making

more complex creations. The carrier board to which you attach the pattern segments allows much more positioning flexibility than you have with template guide routing. (We made the TEMPLATE ROUTING sign *above* using this technique.)

Making your template—the vital first step

Actually, if you do a good job of making your template, you can hardly go wrong after that. So exercise great care at this stage the router will do the rest for you.

Both hardboard and plywood—¼" thick—worked well for us in the shop, but we finally settled on plywood for our templates because it seemed to hold up better over time than did the hardboard. It also was easier for us to see our pattern marks on the plywood.

How to transfer a pattern onto a template blank

If you're lucky enough to have a full-size pattern to work from, just spray some artist's adhesive onto a piece of template material and adhere the pattern to it. If you're working with a scaled drawing, you might just as well recreate the pattern right on the template material as shown in photo A *below.*

Remember that when you use template guides, you need to offset the lines of the pattern as shown in *continued*

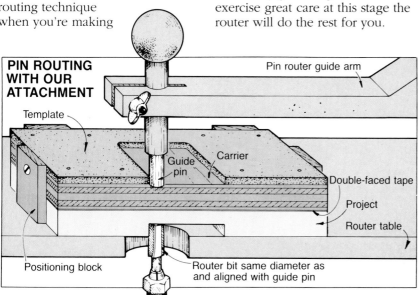

PIN ROUTING WITH OUR ATTACHMENT

Pin router guide arm

Template

Guide pin

Carrier

Double-faced tape

Project

Router table

Positioning block

Router bit same diameter as and aligned with guide pin

A

TEMPLATE ROUTING
continued

the sketch *below* to account for the pattern offset. (The Section View shows how the guide rides against the template.)

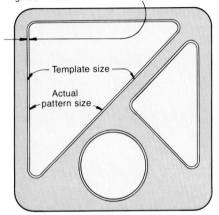

Pattern offset = diameter of template guide − diameter of router bit ÷ 2

Template size

Actual pattern size

ALLOWING FOR PATTERN OFFSET

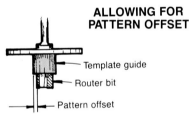

Template guide

Router bit

Pattern offset

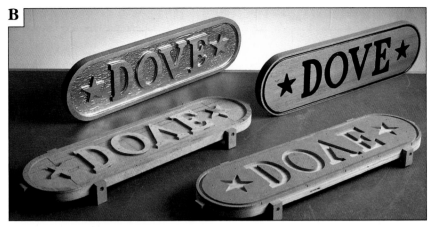

B

C

D

E

Cutting the template

During the research phase of this article, something profoundly simple, but not very obvious, dawned on us. In photo B, *top right,* we have two finished signs with the corresponding template in front of each. Note that if you want to create a raised image, you need a raised template. But if you're working with a recessed design, cut that part of the template away.

Note: *You cut the template material the same no matter whether you're pin routing or using template guides. But keep in mind that template guide routing requires that you leave an extra inch all around the pattern so you can attach the template to the positioning blocks. If pin routing, make the template and carrier the same size as the work.*

Try to machine as much of the template as possible—you'll be much more accurate that way. Drill curved areas with drill bits and circle cutters. And once you've done that, use a saber saw or a scrollsaw to cut within ¼" of the straight lines (we show both of these operations in photos C and D, *opposite center).*

To true up the straight lines, tack a straight piece of scrap wood to the template material as shown in photo E, *opposite bottom*. Place one edge of the straightedge on the pattern line. Then, using a flush-trimming router bit, shear off the excess material.

And to smooth out any minor irregularities, sand all edges. As you can see in photo F, *above right,* we use sandpaper-covered dowels for the corners and a flat sanding block for the straightaways. (We purch-ased automotive-type adhesive-backed aluminum oxide abrasive from a local auto supply house.)

Also, check to see if there are any voids in the edges of the template material, as these can cause you problems when the router guide passes those points. Fill all voids with 5-minute epoxy mixed with sawdust, as shown in photo G at *right*. You'll find this same technique helpful if you happen to nick the template while routing.

Now, if you're template guide routing, drill small guide holes near each end of each side of the template material (you want the holes inside but touching the perimeter lines). Then, using the bit as a guide, as shown in the sketch at *right,* slide the positioning blocks into position under the template material, one side at a time, and nail the template to the blocks.

For pin router projects, position the template on the carrier, pat-tern side down, then nail it (or the several pieces that make up the template) to the carrier. Believe us, it's easy to get confused when positioning the template on the carrier. We found that to read the template from the bottom—like the router bit does when it's cutting—you need to view it

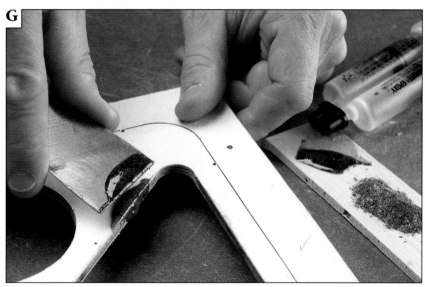

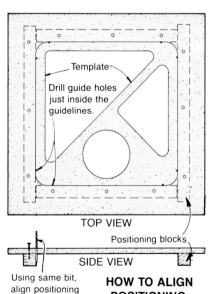

Template

Drill guide holes just inside the guidelines.

TOP VIEW

Positioning blocks

SIDE VIEW

Using same bit, align positioning blocks with guide lines.

HOW TO ALIGN POSITIONING BLOCKS

in a mirror, as shown in photo H, *above right*. (We thought of this only after we laid out a carving

board template backward, which just goes to show you that necessity is definitely the mother of invention.)

Routing your project—the template guide method

Start by fitting your router subbase with the same template guide you used to figure the pattern offset. (We made a large-
continued

TEMPLATE ROUTING
continued

diameter clear acrylic base to allow the router to span the template openings.) Keep in mind that the sleeve portion of the guide must be as short as, or shorter than, the thickness of the template material. (Since we were using ¼" stock, we cut a hole in a scrap piece of template material to accommodate the guide, inserted the sleeve into the hole, and ground the sleeve flush with the template.)

Now, referring to the Router Bit box at *far right,* select the appropriate bit for your project, and set the depth of cut to ¼" or less as shown in photo I, *above right.* You'll find that making several shallow passes is much easier on the router. And, you don't run near the risk of shaking the bit loose and causing deeper-than-desired cuts.

You'll need both hands to control the router, so use double-faced tape to hold the work securely to the work surface. After positioning the template over the workpiece, tip the router bit into the work as shown in photo J at *right.* (We were careful to keep the bit away from the edge of the cutout.)

The sketch at *far right* shows the cutting sequences to follow when you rout out the recesses. First, cut around the perimeter of each recess. Then rout the field area with the grain. If you use a pointed or a rounded router bit to clean the field area, the finished surface will look hand-carved. For a smoother surface, fit a larger-diameter template guide into the router subbase to increase the offset, and clean the field with a straight or mortising bit.

Note: *The 3-in-1 bit shown in the chart will produce a straight wall radiused into a flat bottom without changing template guides.*

Wood chips pile up in a hurry when hollowing out recesses. To keep track of your progress and to prevent chips from building up in corners, a situation that can hamper

cutting performance, stop periodically and blow out the accumulation. And when you're through routing, you'll need to clean up any remaining router marks with a sharp wood chisel and sandpaper.

Routing your project—the pin router method

To employ this technique, you'll need either an overarm pin router or the Delta-Wing Pin Routing Attachment we show you how to build on *pages 75–77.*

To set up our Delta-Wing Pin Routing Attachment, first insert the required number of spacers between the router table and the arm of the attachment. You'll want to position the arm slightly above the template. Now, fit the alignment pin through the opening at the end of the arm and insert it into the router collet. Tighten the wingnuts

ROUTER BITS USED FOR TEMPLATE WORK			
BIT		**SIZES**	**USES**
Straight		⅛-¾"	Cuts flat bottoms, square with walls.
Mortising		½, ¾"	Same as straight, but cuts smoother bottom.
Veining Core box		⅛-¾"	Cuts round-bottom grooves. If used to cut field areas, it leaves a bottom that looks like it was carved with a gouge.
V-grooving		¼, ½, ¾"	Decorative cuts; good for recessed letters.
Bottoming		½, ⅝, ¾"	Use to smooth up bottoms already routed with another bit.
3-in-1		⁷⁄₁₆, ¾"	Cuts a straight wall radiused into a flat bottom.
Keyhole		⅜"	Cuts a flat bottom with a lip overhanging on the side wall. Use for keyhole slots and recessed drawer pulls.
Pilot pan		¼"	Use with guide bushings only. Cuts openings through thin panels and plastic laminates.

ROUTING OUT RECESSES USING TEMPLATE GUIDES

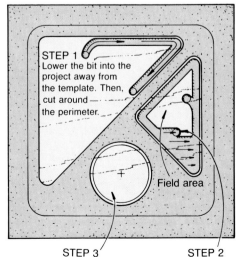

STEP 1
Lower the bit into the project away from the template. Then, cut around the perimeter.

Field area

STEP 3
Clean up router marks with a sharp wood chisel and sandpaper.

STEP 2
Rout field area with the grain.

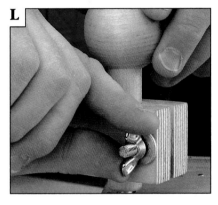

beneath the spacers to secure the attachment directly over the router collet as shown in photo K *above.*

With this done, remove the alignment pin and insert a guide pin into the hole in the arm. This pin must be the same diameter as the router bit you'll use.

Lower the collet to below the work surface, and raise the arm. Then slide the template, carrier board, and workpiece into position, and lock the guide pin so it fits

snugly against the carrier (see photo L at *left).* Now, raise the arm and slide the template out of the way.

Select a router bit that's the same diameter as the guide pin, and tighten it in the collet. Now, raise the bit up to a cutting height of ¼" or less, position the work over the router bit, start the router, and slowly lower the work onto the spinning bit. Note that the guide pin needs to be in one of the recesses in the template to control the cutting action (see photo M *above).* Once you have the work flat on the work surface, flip the hold-down into its closed position. (This lever prevents the guide pin

from jumping up and out of its recess.)

The sketch *below left* shows the cutting sequence to use when pin routing. Here again, rout the perimeter first, then outline any shapes, and clean the field area with the grain. To prevent mishaps such as chip-out at corners and damage to the template, be sure to slow down at corners, and don't slam against the template at the ends of cuts.

The same advice we gave earlier for cleaning up the bottom of the recesses applies when using the pin-routing attachment, too. A rounded or pointed router bit will yield a hand-carved look, whereas a straight or bottoming bit will result in a much smoother surface. Keep in mind that changing to a larger diameter guide pin and a smaller- diameter straight bit allows you to clean the field area without cutting away the coved edges.

ROUTING TECHNIQUES USING THE PIN ROUTING ATTACHMENT

Router bit rotation using router table.

STEP 1
Rout perimeter and outline shapes.

STEP 2
Rout the field area with the grain.
(Note: Don't slam against template at ends of cuts.)

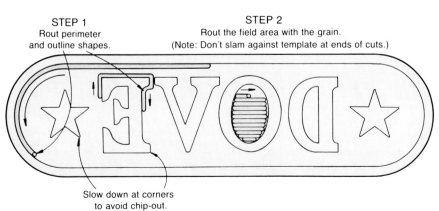

Slow down at corners to avoid chip-out.

MAKE 'EM YOURSELF MOLDINGS

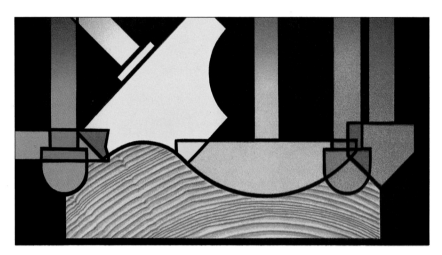

Armed with a router, router table, and a few bits, you can turn plain stock—of any species you want—into custom moldings for a fraction of the cost of milled ones.

If you've ever purchased cabinet-quality moldings, you know that they can cost a bundle. And, you can't always locate the exact molding profile you need for your project. Most outlets that handle moldings stock only the most commonly used designs in the most popular species—pine, oak, poplar, and mahogany.

Of course, woodworkers who own a shaper and a good complement of cutters have no problems making their own moldings. But we've been curious for some time about whether or not it really makes any sense to mill decorative moldings with a router.

To find out, we asked Design Editor Jim Downing to develop five attractive, useful molding profiles to test-make in the shop. Then, once the design work was finished, we rounded up the necessary bits and headed for the router table.

What did we find out during our shop test? Two things, actually. First, if you work carefully, you can, indeed, get good results. And, you can have a lot of fun doing it.

On the following pages we show you exactly how we made our five decorative moldings. Try making one or more of them to get a feel for how the multiple-pass procedure works. Then, once you get the hang of it, try making a few moldings of your own design.

Here's what you'll need to make the moldings

We recommend at least a 1-hp router. You'll also need a router table with a 90° fence 3" to 4" high. The chair rail molding on *page 43* also requires a 45° fence for one of the cuts (see drawing on *page 43* for details on making one).

We chose standard, commonly available bits to make most of the cuts. But several cuts require specialized Sears bits (specified in the instructions). You can substitute similar bits from another manufacturer, but you may have to make some slight adjustments to the bit height and fence locations shown on the drawings.

Tips on making the cuts

1. For each molding, follow the step-by-step drawings to set the bit height and fence position for each pass (we also specify which bits to use). To orient yourself to the end-view drawings, face the router table so the fence is to your right.

Note: In the drawings we include a reference dot (*) to help you identify the position of the piece

2. For a few of the cuts, you'll need support strips to steady the workpiece while routing. Make them the length of the table, and attach them with double-faced tape.

3. Support the ends of long pieces with auxiliary table supports or rollers. Use a feather board to hold the stock against the fence.

4. You'll get more uniform results in grain pattern and color if you make all your molding from the same board.

5. Allow about 6" waste for each 8' of material. You're more likely to dip the stock into the bit or move it away from the fence at the beginning or end of the cut.

6. When making each pass, don't rely entirely on the measurements on drawings. Double-check the bit position against the previous cut to make sure they're perfectly aligned. (We sometimes had to make adjustments in the fence position or bit height because the previous cut was slightly off.) Use a short piece of stock to test bit and fence positions for each pass.

7. If you're making several lengths of the same type of molding, be sure to run all lengths through each step before changing settings.

Table edging

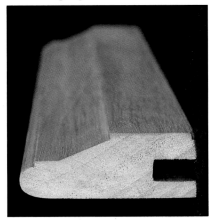

This edging fits tables with ¾"-thick tops. A ¼"×½" slot in the back edge of the molding enables you to spline-join it to the top.

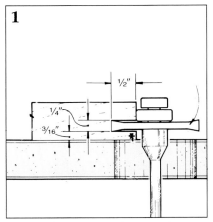

1 Start with ¾×2⅛" stock. Use a ¼" slotcutter bit to rout a groove along one edge of the piece, where shown on the drawing.

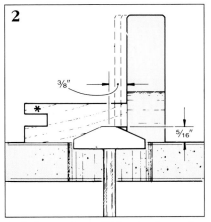

2 Switch to a Sears 1⁷⁄₁₆" raised-panel bit no. 25465. Make three passes by repositioning fence in ⅛" increments.

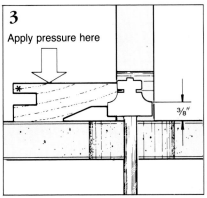

3 Apply pressure here

Switch to a ³⁄₁₆" round-over bit with pilot. While cutting, push down on back side of stock to keep it from rocking.

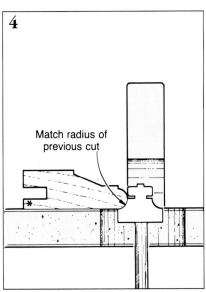

4 Match radius of previous cut

Flip the piece end-for-end. Lower bit to match radius of previous cut. (Do not change the fence position.)

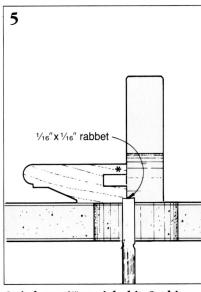

5 ¹⁄₁₆" x ¹⁄₁₆" rabbet

Switch to a ¼" straight bit. Set bit height and fence position to cut a ¹⁄₁₆"×¹⁄₁₆" rabbet. Flop piece as shown.

Base moldings

This popular design adapts well to walls and furniture pieces. Try this easy-to-make molding for starters: it takes only two bits and five cuts.

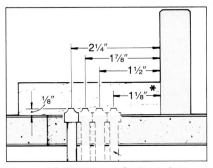

2¼"
1⅞"
1½"
1⅛"
⅛"

Start with ¾×3½" stock. Use a ⅜" beading bit to make cuts where shown by moving the fence.

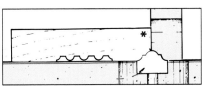

Make the final cut with a ¾" classical bit centered on front edge of fence, as shown on the drawing.

continued

MAKE 'EM YOURSELF MOLDINGS
continued

Picture frame

Beauty often lies in simplicity. As intricate as this decorative picture frame molding looks, you need only two bits to make it: a ½" straight bit and a ¾" ogee bit. And therein lies much of its beauty.

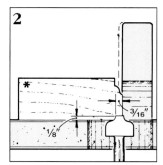

1

Start with 1⅟₁₆ × 2¾" stock. Use a ¾" ogee bit to make cuts for steps 1 through 3.

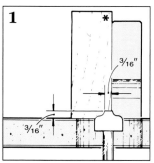

2

Make two passes by moving fence to keep top of bit from chipping out the wood.

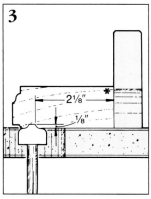

3

Flip the piece end-for-end. To make the cut, align bit with radius of previous cut.

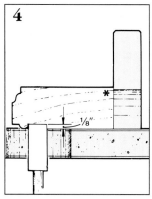

4

Use a ½" straight bit. Set fence and bit height so bit cuts flush with corner of bead.

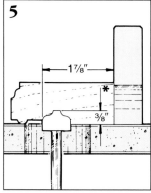

5

Switch back to the ¾" ogee bit to make this cut. You may need to make two passes.

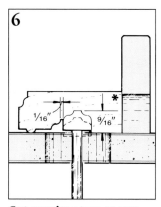

6

Cut requires two passes. Raise bit to full height to set fence, then lower to make first pass.

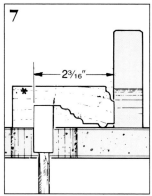

7

Flip piece end-for-end. Set ½" straight bit to match height of previous cut, as shown.

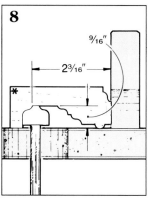

8

Switch back to the ¾" ogee bit, setting its height to match that of the previous cut.

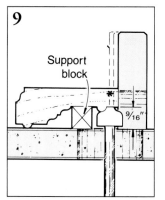

9

Attach a ½ × ⁹⁄₁₆"-high support block to table where shown. Make three passes.

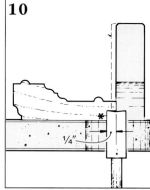

10

Position the ½" straight bit to cut a ¼ × ¼" rabbet. Move fence; make two passes.

Continuous drawer pull

Continuous pulls make a popular alternative to hardware on the doors and drawers of contemporary cabinets and other furniture. We've designed this one to fit standard ½" laminated plywood or particleboard drawer fronts.

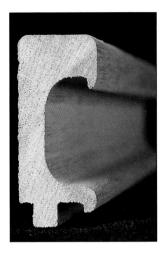

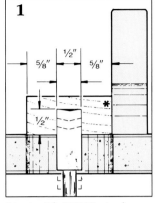

1

Start with ¾X1¾" stock. Use a ½" straight bit. Make three passes by raising bit.

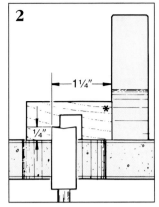

2

Lower bit to ¼" above table height, and reposition fence to make cut where shown.

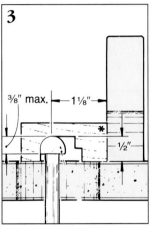

3

Flip the piece end-for-end. Use a ½" core box bit with a *maximum* profile height of ⅜".

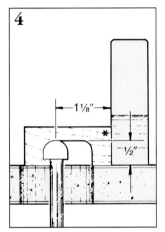

4

Flip piece end-for-end. Do not change bit height or fence position when making this cut.

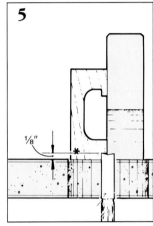

5

Use a ¼" straight bit, centered on front face of fence, to cut the rabbet where shown.

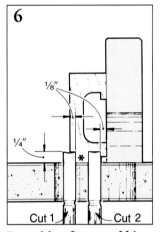

6

Reposition fence and bit where shown on drawing to make cut 1; again to make cut 2.

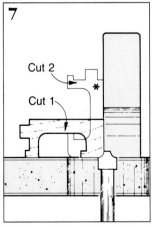

7

Align radius of ⅜" beading bit with face of fence to round over outside corners as shown.

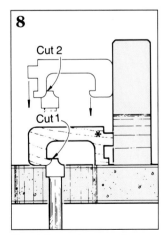

8

Reset fence to round over inside corners of pull (cuts 1 and 2). Do not change bit height.

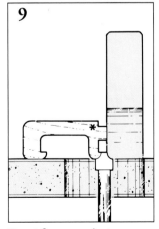

9

Reset fence again to round over bottom lip of pull as shown. Do not reset bit height.

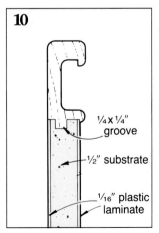

10

To install, rout a ¼X¼" groove in top edge of door or drawer front. Glue pull in place.

continued

41

MAKE 'EM YOURSELF MOLDINGS

continued

Picture rail

You'll most often see this molding in older homes with tall ceilings. Running horizontally about 2' below the ceiling, the rail forms a lip for hanging pictures (or displaying china plates). You'll need a table saw to do step 6.

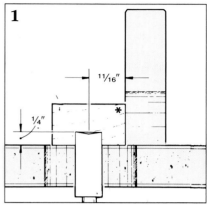

1

Start with ¾×1⅜" stock. Use a ½" straight bit to cut a ¼"-deep groove in the center of the piece.

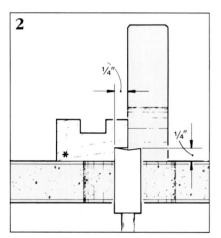

2

Without changing the bit height, move the fence to center its front face above the router bit, as shown.

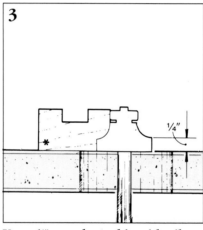

3

Use a ¼" round-over bit, with pilot bearing. You won't need the router table fence for this step.

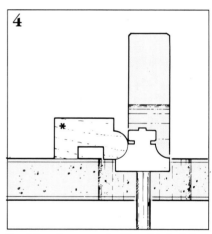

4

Position fence and adjust bit height to align bit so it matches radius of cut you made in previous step.

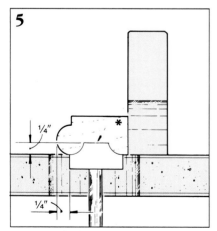

5

Remove the bit's pilot bearing to make this cut. Align bit with radius of cut you made in previous step.

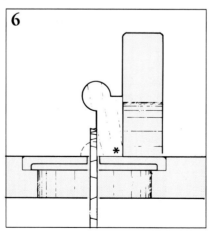

6

On your table saw, cut off the lower projection on the piece where shown on the drawing, to make a flush edge.

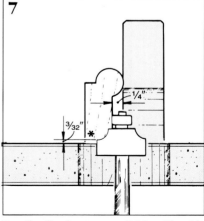

7

For the final cut, use a ³⁄₁₆" beading bit (with pilot). Set fence to support the piece, as shown on the drawing.

Chair rail

Use this molding as a decorative accent on walls—and to keep the backs of chairs and other furniture from marring wall coverings. Typically, you'd run this molding horizontally, 32–36" above floor level. You'll need a 45° fence to make the second cut.

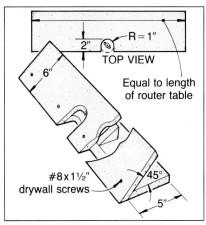

You'll need a 45° fence on your router table to make this molding. We made the one pictured here from ¾" particleboard.

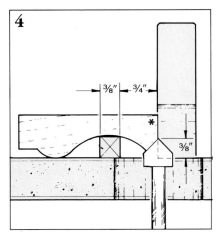

1 Use Sears 1" radius end-cove bit no. 25526. Start with ¾×2¾" stock. Make three passes.

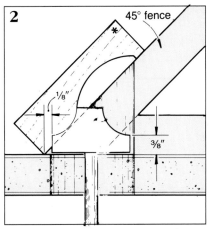

2 Use Sears ½" round-over bit without pilot. Switch to a 45° fence like the one shown in the drawing *top right*.

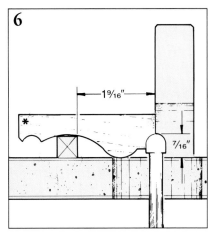

3 Switch back to a 90° fence. Use a ¼" straight bit; align it to bottom edge of the radius made in step 2.

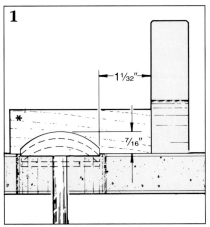

4 Attach a ⁷⁄₁₆×⁷⁄₁₆" support strip to the table where shown. Chamfer edge with a ⅜" V-grooving bit.

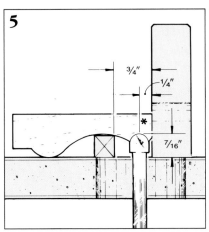

5 Leave support strip in the same position. Reposition fence and make cut with a ⅜" core box bit.

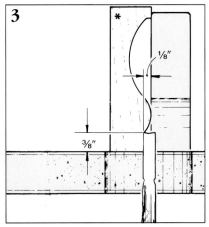

6 Flip piece end-for-end, reposition support strip and fence, and make cut with same bit used for step 5.

TAMBOUR

First used in France during the 17th century, the tambour gained acclaim in the U.S. when the rolltop desk skyrocketed in popularity during the late 1800s. Nowadays, you can add a fashionable and functional accent to your projects with this time-honored alternative to hinged doors.

Whether you're building a breadbox, video cabinet, or appliance garage, a tambour curtain adds a special charm to your project. Unlike hinged doors, a tambour curtain won't swing open into nearby objects.

To guide you through nearly any tambour project, we'll show you how to plan, build, and install a vertical curtain such as the one in the countertop appliance garage shown *above*.

To build a horizontal curtain, follow the same procedures described here, but remember that the tracks for the tambour will be in the top and bottom panels of the cabinet, not the ends.

Plan now for smooth rolling later

All tambour curtains ride in narrow tracks and consist of slats of wood held together with a canvas backing. To help you build this

kind of curtain into your next project, we developed this simple planning procedure.

With your cabinet dimensions in hand, determine the sizes of the tambour slats and the tracks by using the chart and drawing *opposite, top*. Note that larger cabinet openings (spans) require thicker and wider tambour slats for rigidity and appearance.

Now, refer to the examples shown *opposite, bottom*, and select the shape of the slats. Keep these considerations in mind for tambours that will prove both attractive *and* practical:

• Rectangular slats add a contemporary touch.

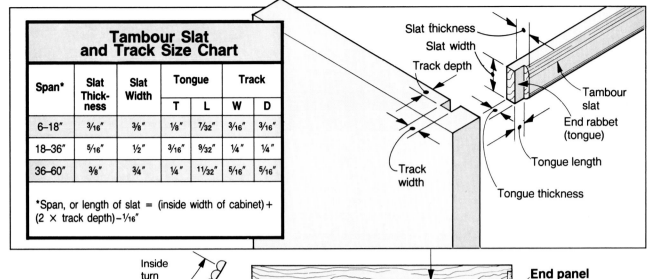

Tambour Slat and Track Size Chart

Span*	Slat Thick-ness	Slat Width	Tongue T	Tongue L	Track W	Track D
6–18"	3/16"	3/8"	1/8"	7/32"	3/16"	3/16"
18–36"	5/16"	1/2"	3/16"	9/32"	1/4"	1/4"
36–60"	3/8"	3/4"	1/4"	11/32"	5/16"	5/16"

*Span, or length of slat = (inside width of cabinet) + (2 × track depth) – 1/16"

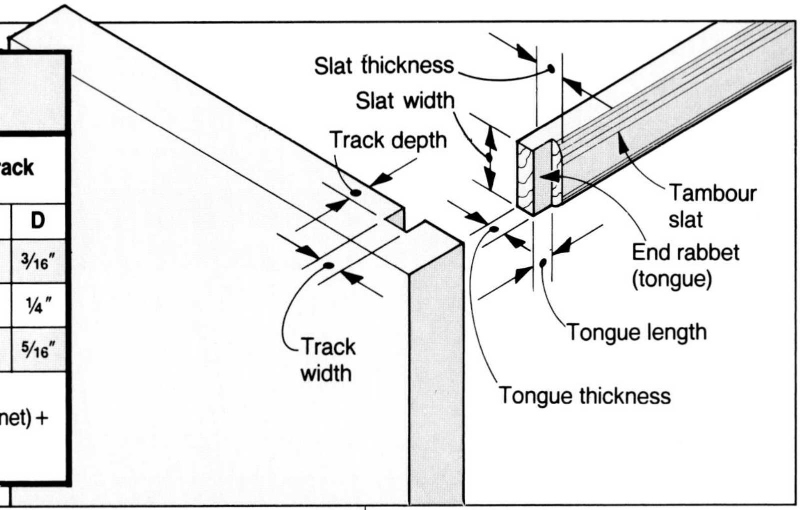

Slat thickness
Slat width
Track depth
Tambour slat
End rabbet (tongue)
Tongue length
Track width
Tongue thickness

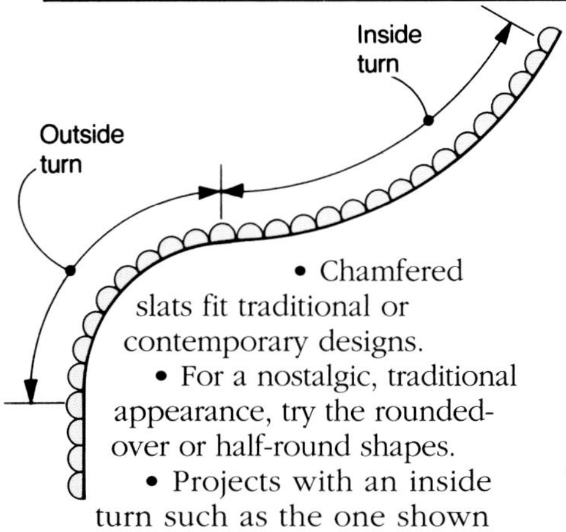

Inside turn
Outside turn

• Chamfered slats fit traditional or contemporary designs.

• For a nostalgic, traditional appearance, try the rounded-over or half-round shapes.

• Projects with an inside turn such as the one shown *above* require a half-round or beveled shape to allow the tambour to make this turn. Remember that inside turns, such as on a rolltop desk, must be gradual. Otherwise, the tambour will not negotiate the turn.

Next, cut a piece of ¾" particleboard to the inside dimensions of your project's end panels for use later as a routing template. On one side of the particleboard, lay out the path of the tambour track by following the guidelines in the drawing *above right* and this procedure:

First, mark the track setbacks for the front, top, and rear. When determining the front setback, remember that your lift bar should be at least as thick as the slats and set at least ⅛" back from the front edge or the cabinet side. Then, draw the tambour track parallel to the front, top, and rear, and mark

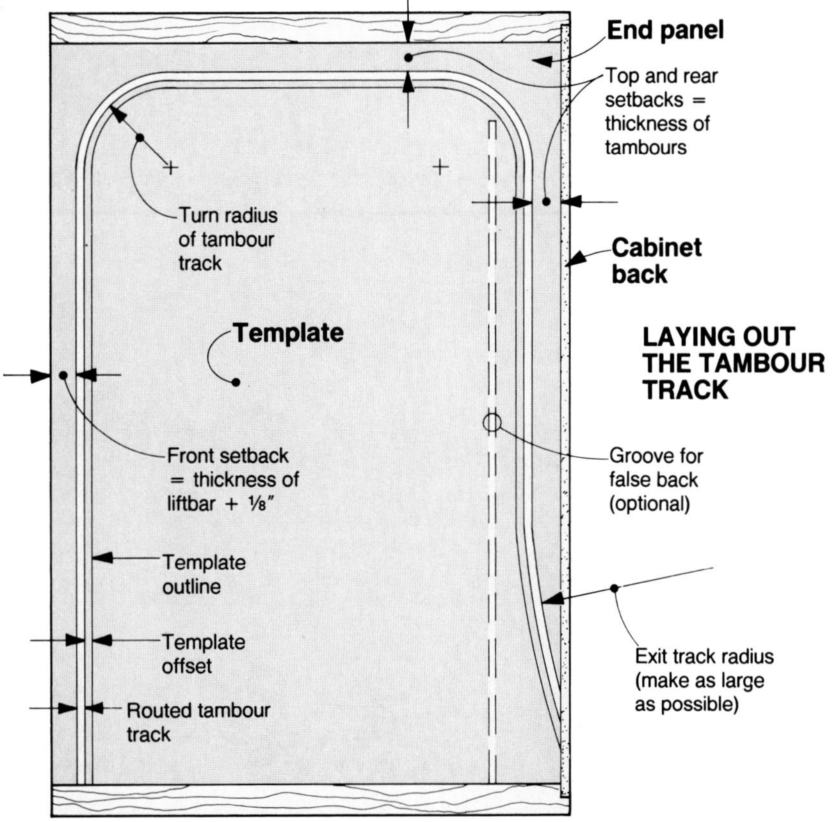

End panel
Top and rear setbacks = thickness of tambours
Turn radius of tambour track
Cabinet back
Template
LAYING OUT THE TAMBOUR TRACK
Front setback = thickness of liftbar + ⅛"
Groove for false back (optional)
Template outline
Template offset
Routed tambour track
Exit track radius (make as large as possible)

continued

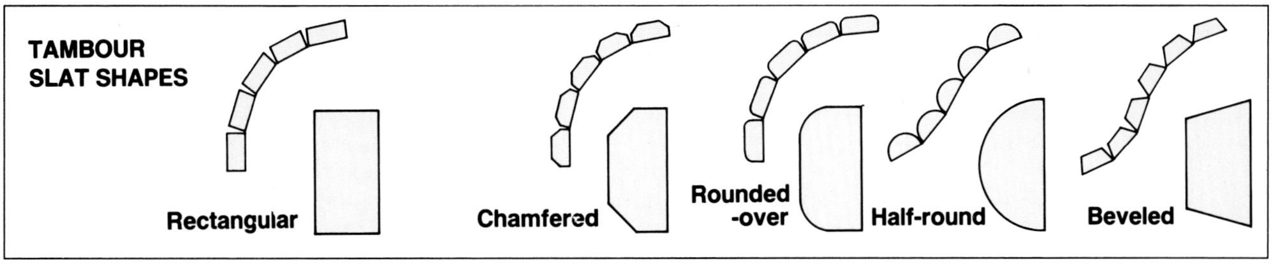

TAMBOUR SLAT SHAPES
Rectangular
Chamfered
Rounded -over
Half-round
Beveled

TAMBOUR
continued

Minimum Track Outside Turn Radius		
Tambour Width		Minimum Radius
⅜"	=	1"
½"	=	1½"
¾"	=	2"

the exit track radius. Using the chart *above,* determine the minimum radius for the outside turns at the top of the panels and connect the corners with a compass.

Next, determine the template offset that corresponds to the guide bushing and

straight bit you'll chuck into your router. For an idea of how the template offset works, see *below.* For example, a ½" guide bushing and a ¼" straight bit will result in a ⅛" template offset. Now, draw the offset just inside and parallel to the track already marked on the particleboard.

If you would like to add a ¼" plywood false back to hide the tambour, see the illustration on *page 45* for the position of a

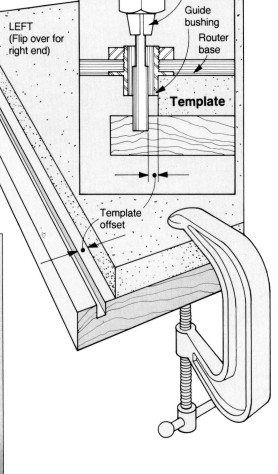

LEFT (Flip over for right end)

Router collet

Guide bushing

Router base

Template

Template offset

holding groove. Lay out this groove directly on the end panels.

Put the cabinet panels on track

To shape the template, bandsaw along the outside of the offset line, being careful not to saw inside the mark. Then, sand to the offset line for a smooth template edge. This template will help you rout tracks on both end panels. Here's how. First, clamp the template to one of the panels and rout the track as shown in the photo and illustration at *left.* Be sure to move the router in a counterclockwise direction for a smooth and crisp cut. Then, flip over the template and repeat this operation for the other end panel. Remove the template and use a straightedge to rout a groove for the false back if necessary. Finally, assemble the cabinet (including the false back).

Note: You must assemble the cabinet squarely or the tambour will not slide smoothly.

Let's build the tambour curtain

For a tambour that's a pleasing, consistent color to the eye, cut all the slats from a single board. You'll want to buy a long board and cut it into several lengths just slightly longer than your slats.

To determine how much material you'll need, first decide how many slats will be required for a curtain that reaches from the bottom of the closure to just past the first turn in the track. Since none of us are perfect (and neither is lumber), it's a good idea to cut four or five extra slats in case some warp or you make a small goof when machining them. Now, add together the thickness of one slat, the saw kerf of your ripping blade, and ⅟₃₂" for a jointer cut, then multiply that figure times the number of slats. That number tells you the total width of lumber you will cut, but keep these things in mind:

• For safety, you can't rip or joint strips from the full width of every board, so start with stock 2" wider than the amount of wood you'll saw from it. This will leave 2" of scrap stock as you machine the last slat from that board.

• Choose a board that's as thick as your slats are wide. Otherwise, be prepared to plane the board to the correct thickness.

To cut the slats, remember these words: joint, rout, sand, and rip. The sequence works like this:

Cut the board into lengths that are 1" or 2" longer than the tambour (including tongues). Joint ½₂" from one edge of the board, and rout the slat shape onto that edge as shown at *right*. Now, sand the shaped surface with 150-grit paper.

Set your tablesaw fence for the thickness of the slats, and with the shaped edge against the fence, rip the board as we're doing *below right,* using the pushblock *below.* Number each slat on the sawn side so you can situate them in the tambour in the same order they came out of the board. Repeat this sequence for each slat, always jointing the sawn edge of the board to re-establish a straight and smooth edge for the next slat. To help you attach a lift bar later, rip two more slats with no routed shape.

continued

Rout slowly to avoid splintering as you shape the tambour slat.

PUSHBLOCK
for ripping
tambour strips

¾ × 3 × 6"
(glue only to base)

Saw kerf

Equal to
thickness
of tambours

¾ × 3 × 8"

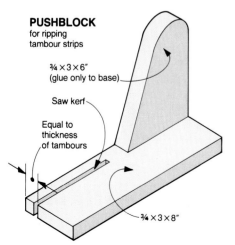

For safety's sake, use a pushblock to rip the tambour slats.

TAMBOUR
continued

To turn that loose pile of sticks into an orderly tambour, first use a framing square to set two cleats at a 90° angle for the gluing jig shown at *right*. After screwing down the cleats, place all the tambour slats (in numbered order), shaped side down onto the jig, and place the two unshaped slats at the bottom. With the slats pressed firmly together, screw the other two cleats in place.

With a piece of pre-washed 10-oz. canvas, cut the material so it covers the slats from top to bottom and centers 1" from both ends (we bought our canvas at a fabric store).

If your finished tambour will be a dark color, treat the canvas with dark brown dye (the type available at grocery and variety stores). Doing so will help prevent the canvas backing from showing between the slats. Make sure the dye dries completely before proceeding.

Then, spread an even layer of white woodworker's glue over the slats and lay the canvas in place. Glue should not squeeze between the slats if you have no large gaps between them. After smoothing out the canvas with a rolling pin, add the waxed paper, particleboard or plywood panel, and weight. Allow the glue to dry for one hour. The tambour will have a slight case of rigor mortis, so break the glue between the slats by running the tambour over a tabletop as we're doing *top, far right*. Trim both ends of the tambour as shown at *center right*.

Now, chuck a straight bit into your router table and set the fence for the tongue length of the tambour. Elevate the bit just ½" above the router table and run the cloth side of the tongue over the bit. This helps even out any irregularities in the thickness of the slats. For this operation, use the pushstick at *right* to hold down

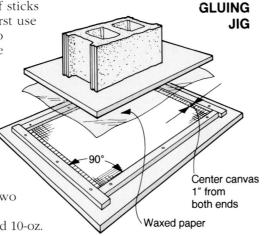

GLUING JIG

90°

Center canvas 1" from both ends

Waxed paper

Use the corner of a tabletop to break the glue between the slats.

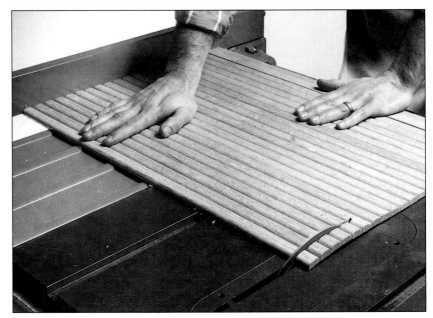

Trim the curtain with your tablesaw and stand to the side of the blade in case it ejects small slat pieces.

PUSHSTICK
for cutting rabbet in slats

Short length of tambour strip glued to bottomside of pushstick

¾ × 3"

Equal to overal height of assembled tambours

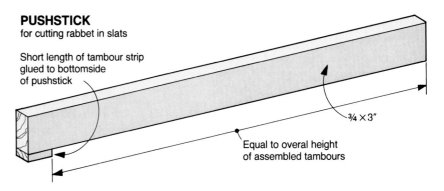

Hold down the tambour firmly when routing the rabbet.

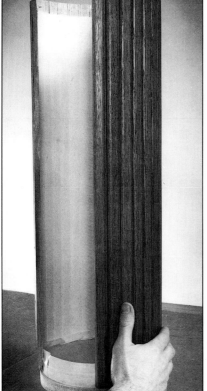

Attach the curtain to a disc with double-faced tape. This helps you apply stain and other finishes between the slats.

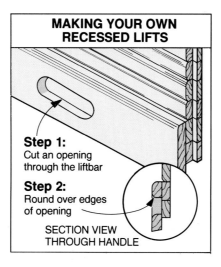

MAKING YOUR OWN RECESSED LIFTS

Step 1:
Cut an opening through the liftbar

Step 2:
Round over edges of opening

SECTION VIEW THROUGH HANDLE

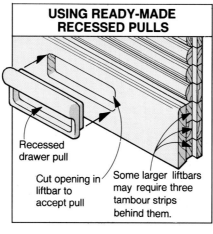

USING READY-MADE RECESSED PULLS

Recessed drawer pull

Cut opening in liftbar to accept pull

Some larger liftbars may require three tambour strips behind them.

the tambour. Next, flip over the curtain, raise the router bit to cut the tongue to the correct thickness, and use the same pushstick to rout the rabbet (see photo at *top left*).

Final curtain call: install the tambour

It's the moment of truth—time to test the tambour for fit. The curtain should slide with just a slight amount of side-to-side play. Ours initially felt tight and jerky, so we lubricated the tongues with some paraffin—beeswax also works. Presto! A smooth-rolling tambour.

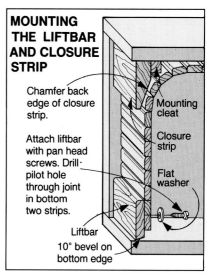

MOUNTING THE LIFTBAR AND CLOSURE STRIP

Chamfer back edge of closure strip.

Attach liftbar with pan head screws. Drill pilot hole through joint in bottom two strips.

Mounting cleat

Closure strip

Flat washer

Liftbar

10° bevel on bottom edge

When you're satisfied with the fit, add a lift bar by using one of the two methods shown at *left*. To attach the lift bar and an optional closure strip, see the illustration *above*. The closure strip hides the turn in the tambour.

Finally, you have several means to stop the tambour from sliding too far back into the cabinet. A solid lift bar coming in contact with a closure strip will do the trick. Or, set one screw into each track at a point where the back end of the tambour will contact the exposed heads of the screws when the lift bar reaches the top of the closure.

To finish the curtain, remove it from the cabinet and attach it with double-faced tape to a scrapwood disc as shown at *far left*. This arrangement allows the stain and finish to reach between the slats.

ROUTER PROJECTS

A router can help you make a Parsons table, carving board,
various serving dishes, and other exciting projects.

PICTURE-PERFECT PARSONS TABLE

A single sheet of ¾" plywood and another of high-gloss laminate join forces in this easy-as-pie project. The finished product measures 36" square and 17" high—ideal for a conversation grouping like this one. Or, adapt our dimensions to suit your specific requirements. If you want another color or finish, today's selection of laminates gives you choices galore.

Building the plywood frame

1. Lay out all the parts of the frame on the face side of the plywood, where shown in the Cutting diagram on *page 52.* Then, with a tablesaw (and helper if you can find one), cut the top (A) to size.

2. Using the Cutting diagram as reference, rough-cut the table legs (B, C) with a jigsaw. Then, trim the exterior edges and the leg bottoms with the tablesaw.

3. To make the interior cuts on B and C easier to cut perfectly straight, attach a long wooden auxiliary fence to your tablesaw fence. Unplug the tablesaw, raise the blade to its full height, and position the fence against the blade. Slide a piece of wood along the fence until it comes into contact with the blade, and mark the maximum length of the blade cut on the wooden fence, as shown in the drawing *above right.* Extend these lines up the side of the wooden fence so that they will be visible when you cut the plywood.

4. Using a straightedge, mark start and stop lines on each A and B, where shown in the Cutting diagram. Now, move the tablesaw fence 2¼" away from the inside edge of the blade. Lower the blade below the surface of the table, and set one of the B legs on the surface

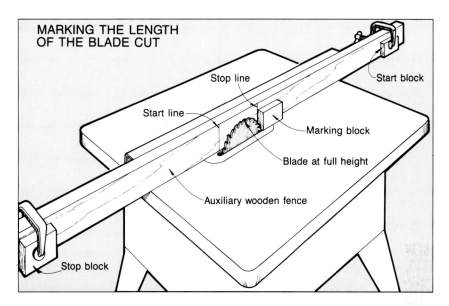

MARKING THE LENGTH OF THE BLADE CUT

Stop line · Start block · Start line · Marking block · Blade at full height · Auxiliary wooden fence · Stop block

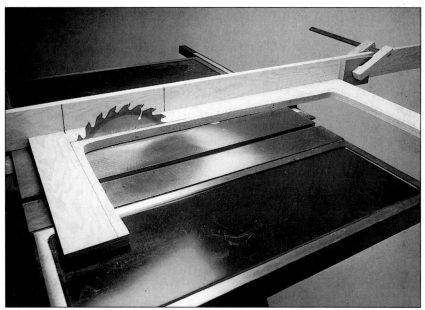

of the saw. Line up the start and stop lines on B with those on the wooden fence, and clamp start and stop blocks to the fence at those points (see the photo *above*).

5. With one of the Bs against the auxiliary fence and the start block, plug the tablesaw in, turn it on. Slowly raise the rotating blade up through the ¾" plywood stock until

the blade is extended upward to its full cutting height. Not only is the blade at its full cutting height, it is at its full cutting length as measured in Step 3.

Warning: *When raising the moving saw blade through the plywood, be sure to hold the plywood firmly against the table,*
continued

PICTURE-PERFECT PARSONS TABLE

continued

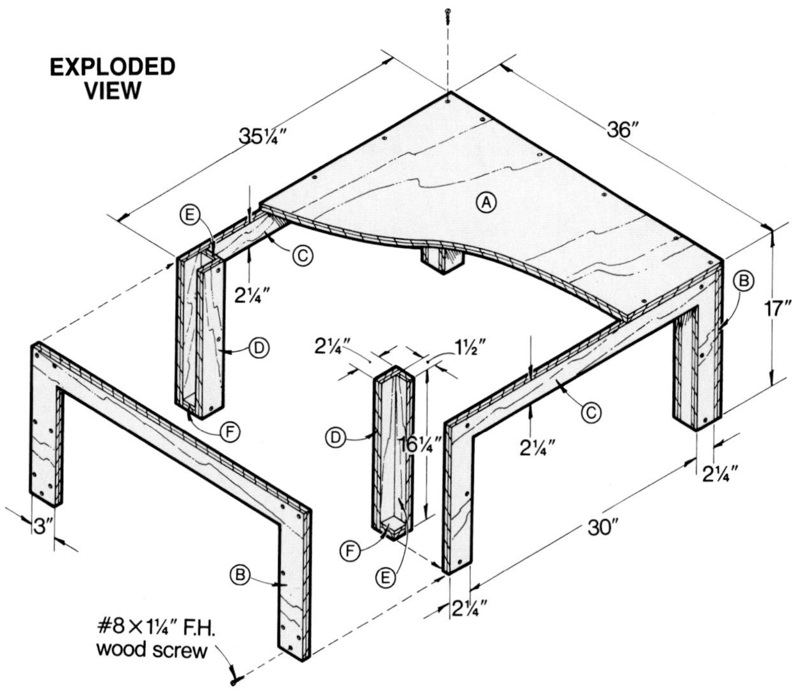
EXPLODED VIEW
35¼″
36″
A
E
C
B
2¼″
17″
D
2¼″
1½″
16¼″
F
D
2¼″
C
2¼″
3″
30″
F
B
E
2¼″
#8 × 1¼″ F.H. wood screw

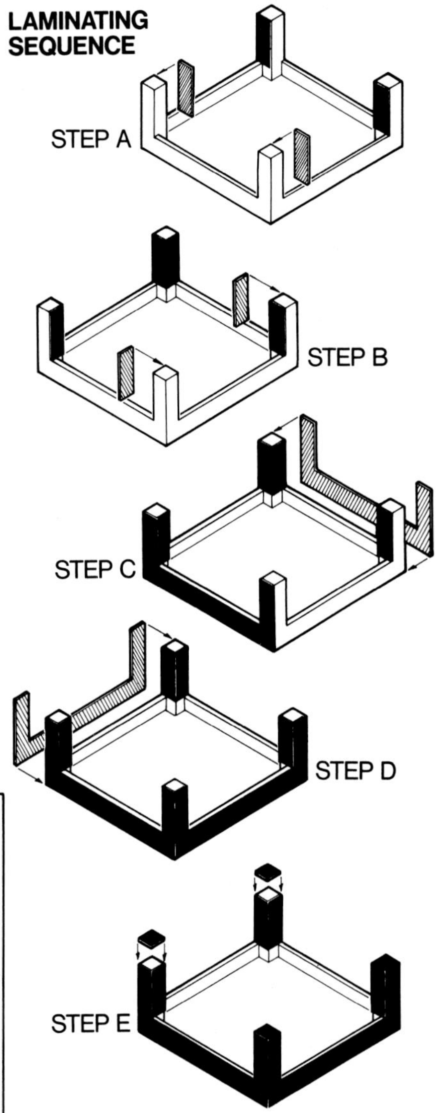
LAMINATING SEQUENCE
STEP A
STEP B
STEP C
STEP D
STEP E

Cutting Diagram

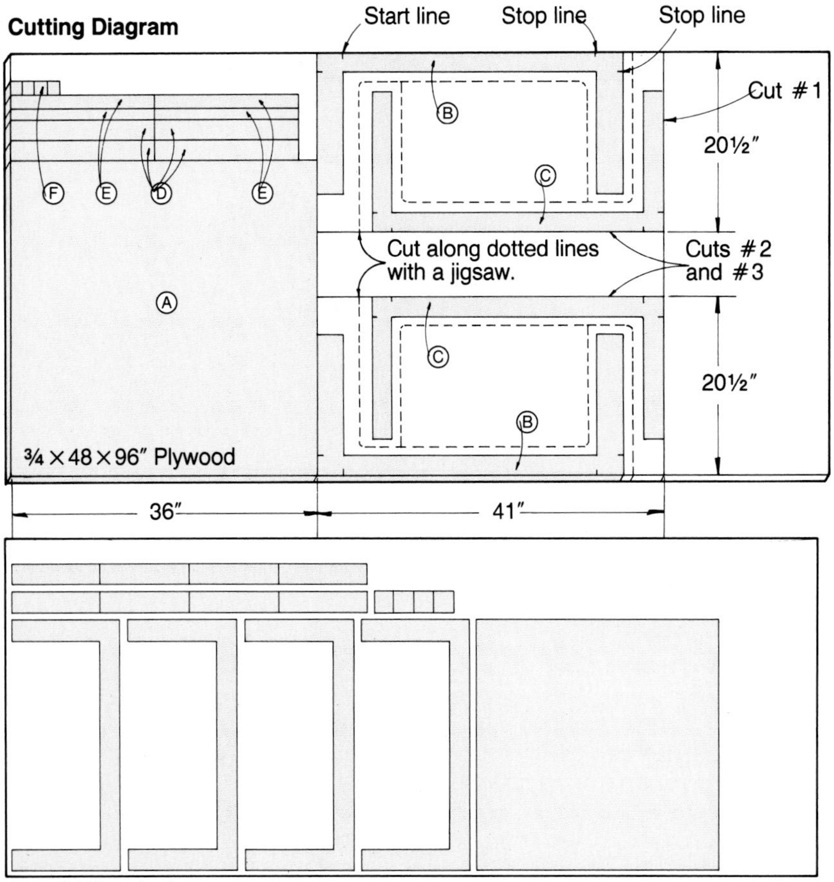
Start line
Stop line
Stop line
Cut #1
B
C
20½″
F
E
D
E
Cut along dotted lines with a jigsaw.
Cuts #2 and #3
A
C
B
20½″
¾ × 48 × 96″ Plywood
36″
41″
48 × 120″ Laminate

Bill of Materials					
Part	Finished Size*			Mat.	Qty.
	T	W	L		
A	¾"	36"	36"	P	1
B*	¾"	16¼"	36"	P	2
C*	¾"	16¼"	34½"	P	2
D	¾"	2¼"	16¼"	P	4
E	¾"	1½"	16¼"	P	4
F	¾"	1½"	1½"	P	4

*These parts are cut larger initially, then trimmed to finished size. Please read the instructions before cutting.

Material Key: P—plywood

Supplies: #8x1¼" flathead wood screws, wood filler, contact cement, plastic laminate, black paint, petroleum jelly, permanent black felt-tipped marker.

but do not put your hand near the area where the blade will protrude!

6. Push the leg along the fence until you meet the stop block at the other end of the fence (see the photo at *right*). Holding B in place, shut off the saw and wait until it comes to a complete stop before removing the piece. Lower the blade, place the other B in position, raise the blade through it, and cut it in the same manner. To cut the C legs (they are ¾" narrower), you will need to move each stop block toward the center by ¾".

7. To make the cuts along the legs of B, move the fence 3" from the inside edge of the blade. Position a stop block on the fence, and cut both inside cuts on each B as shown in the drawing at *right*. Move the fence 2¼" from the blade, and make both cuts on the inside edge of each C using the same stop block. You will need to use a handsaw to square up the cuts, as the blade leaves an arc-shaped cut.

8. Dry-clamp the leg assemblies (B-C) together, and check for a proper fit of all the parts. Trim if necessary. Then, glue and clamp the leg assemblies together, checking for square. Be careful not to round over or dent the square edges when clamping. To reinforce the joints, drill pilot holes and drive #8x1¼" flathead wood screws where shown in the Exploded View drawing *opposite*. Make sure the head of each screw rests flush with the surface of the plywood (otherwise they will show through when you apply the laminate).

9. Glue and clamp the tabletop onto the leg assembly, and secure it with screws.

10. Cut the plywood parts D, E, and F to the sizes given in the Bill of Materials for the inner legs. Glue up one D, one E, and one F for each inner leg. Secure the pieces together with #8x1¼" flathead wood screws.

11. Glue and screw the inner-leg assemblies to the table assembly to form the completed carcass.

12. After the glue dries, fill *all* voids and holes with filler. Sand the carcass assembly smooth, being

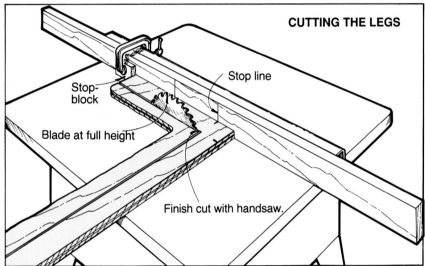

CUTTING THE LEGS

Stop-block

Stop line

Blade at full height

Finish cut with handsaw.

extremely careful not to round-over any edges.

Applying the laminate

Note: If you don't have any experience with applying plastic laminate, or you're a little rusty, read these techniques, as well as those on pages 54–58.

1. Using the Laminating Sequence drawing *opposite* as a guide, cut and apply laminate to the inner edges of each leg (see Steps A and B).

2. Lower the table onto the face side of the laminate, and trace the outline of the legs and tabletop with a colored grease pencil. Allow at least ½" in all directions when cutting for overlap, as it will be trimmed with a router later.

Apply the laminate to the plywood legs as shown in Steps C and D, then to the tabletop, and then to the bottom of the legs (Step E). Trim after each step with a router fitted with a flush-trimming bit. (We rubbed petroleum jelly along the path of the bit's pilot to prevent it from marring the already-applied laminate. The pilot may clog with glue and burn the laminate.)

3. To minimize the seam lines of the laminate, "stain" the exposed laminate edges with a permanent black felt-tipped marker. Wipe off the excess with a clean rag.

4. Mask off the laminate and paint the remaining exposed plywood on the bottom side of the table black.

continued

PICTURE-PERFECT PARSONS TABLE
continued

Project Tool List
Tablesaw
Portable jigsaw
Router
   Bits: ¼" flush-trimming bit

Note: *We built the project using the tools listed You may be able to substitute other tools or equipment for listed items you don't have. Additional common hand tools and clamps may be required to complete the project.*

APPLYING PLASTIC LAMINATES

To assist you in applying a plastic laminate on your Parsons table, we've divided this section into two parts. "The Basics" will serve as a refresher for those of you who have some experience with plastic laminate already (and as an introduction for those who don't). In "Nifty Solutions for Special Situations" we deal with some situations and some new materials you may not have encountered yet.

THE BASICS:
Two good ways to cut laminate down to size ·

1. The score-and-snap method of cutting laminate works well with all standard laminates, but not with solid-core surfacing materials. Start by laying the laminate face up on a clean surface. Then, mark the cutoff lines, allowing at least ½" in both directions for overhang. Put a piece of thin scrap beneath the cutoff line, locate the straightedge so that it protects the panel you'll be using, then score along a straightedge several times with a sharp-pointed tool as shown in photo A. We use an inexpensive carbide-tipped scoring tool we bought at a local floor-covering tool supplier. When you see the dark

backing showing through the color layer the entire length of the cutoff line, you're there.

2. With your hands positioned as shown in photo B and with the laminate face up, lift up on one end of the laminate, exerting pressure until the material snaps. The photo inset shows what happens at the score line (a) if you press down on the laminate rather than lift up; (b) if you do as we suggest; and (c) if you don't score the laminate completely.

With today's newer solid-color surfacing materials, you can create an array of striking edging treatments. Here we combined a walnut banding with Formica-brand "pale gold" solid-color surfacing material, then routed a cove along the top edge.

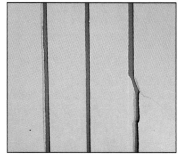

3. In situations where you need to cut the laminate in two or more directions, lay out and mark the cutoff lines, then drill a small hole in the scrap portion where the cutoff lines intersect as shown in photo C. Doing this prevents you from accidentally scoring too far and also lessens the chance of stress cracks developing at the corner. Score completely through the shortest dimension, then score and snap along the other.

4. We've also had good luck cutting laminate with a router fitted with a flush trimming bit. Just mark your cutoff line, clamp a straightedge beneath the laminate, and run the router along the straightedge as shown in photo D. You'll get a super-smooth cut.

Preparing the surface for plastic laminate

We've used both good-quality plywood and particleboard as a substrate for laminate. Regardless of which material you use, though, fill surface voids before applying the laminate. Also true up the edges and fill voids with wood putty.

Photo E shows the setup we use to guarantee a smooth edge. This technique comes in handy if you plan to band the edges of a panel with wood.

When putting an edge banding on a shelf or countertop (see photo F), glue and nail the wood to the substrate, making sure the top edge of the banding is slightly higher than the substrate. Go back later and either plane or scrape the surfaces flush. Don't use a belt sander; it may gouge the surface or round over an edge.

Applying the adhesive and laminate

1. Because you want to minimize the visual impact of the joint lines, the sequence of application is every bit as important as the technique. As a general rule, cover the underside of a panel first, the back and side edges, the front edge, and finish with the top surface. Contact

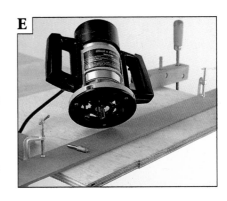

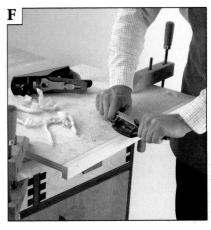

cement sets up quickly, so on all but very small projects we recommend using a narrow, short-napped roller as shown in photo G. Give both mating surfaces one liberal coat of contact cement (use
continued

PICTURE-PERFECT PARSONS TABLE
continued

only the non-flammable type), then allow the adhesive to dry. How do you know when the surfaces are ready for contact? Give them the touch test! If the adhesive sticks to your finger when you touch it, it's not ready.

2. To keep from mispositioning the laminate on the substrate, we lay venetian blind slats between the substrate and the laminate as shown in photo H. Once we have laid the laminate into position and have checked to make sure we have excess to trim off on all edges, we withdraw the slats one at a time. Smooth the laminate with one hand as you work toward the other end.

3. If for some reason you goof, we've found that you can retrieve laminate even if it's already made contact. With a spray bottle partially full of contact, spray a fine mist of solvent along the edge as shown in photo I. Then, lift up the edge with a putty knife. Continue spraying and lifting, and the substrate and laminate will part company. Allow the solvent to evaporate, recoat both the laminate and substrate, and relay the laminate.

4. After the substrate and laminate make contact, you want to ensure a good bond between the two. Though you can accomplish this by tapping the entire surface with a scrap block and hammer, we use a rubber J-roller. With it, we can apply a lot of pressure, and we also avoid the problem of fracturing the laminate at the edges (see photo J), which is a possibility with the other method.

Trimming and finishing off the edges

We've trimmed laminate with carbide-tipped flush-trimming router bits with ball-bearing pilots, but we can honestly say that a much less expensive solid carbide bit with a solid pilot works just as well for us. And that's the opinion of some professionals we've talked

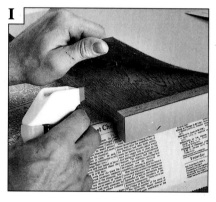

to as well. With either type bit, you've got to be on guard against burning or scratching adjoining surfaces. We've found the two best strategies here are to keep the router moving and to apply a layer of petroleum jelly to the surface that the bearing guides against before routing off the excess (see photo K). Theoretically, a router bit with a ball bearing guide should prevent mishaps. But as you trim an edge, for example, the contact cement builds up and restricts the movement of the bearing.

Trimming laminates with a flush trimming bit results in a sharp, square edge. For safety's sake, dress the edge with a single-cut file as shown in photo L. Hold the file so that the edge will be beveled slightly, and move the file across the edge lightly several times.

More tips on working with laminates

- Before working with plastic laminate or the newer solid-color surfacing materials, allow a day or so for the material to acclimate. Also make sure that the contact cement is at room temperature before applying it.

- Be *extra* careful when handling and working the solid-color surfacing materials. They're even more brittle than standard laminates. They also have the habit of chipping when being cut, so use sharp, carbide-tipped cutters when cutting or shaping them. And if you glue several layers of these materials together to create decorative edge treatments, be sure to scuff up the face of the layers to which other material will be applied to ensure a good bond.

- If you apply laminate to any surface that won't be anchored securely to another assembly, always apply laminate, or the less-expensive "backing sheet," to the back side of the panel to minimize the chances of warping due to moisture.

- Always work in a well-ventilated area when applying contact cement, as its vapors can be dizzying if inhaled for too long a period. And don't work around heat or flames.

- Sometimes air bubbles form between the laminate and the substrate after application and cause the bond to break. (Usually the cause of this is laying down the laminate before the cement has "flashed off.") To correct this situation, lay a damp cloth over the area in question, then place an iron set at the cotton setting onto the cloth. Doing this reactivates the cement and allows you to press the laminate and substrate together.

- To help prevent stress cracks at inside corners, hold the contact cement back about 6" in all directions from the corner, then apply white glue to both surfaces and clamp them together.

- To keep the contact cement applicator relatively pliable between coats, wrap it in plastic to keep the solvent from escaping.

NIFTY SOLUTIONS FOR SPECIAL SITUATIONS: Wrapping laminate around corners

Ever wonder if you could wrap plastic laminate around a relatively tight radius? We were curious to find out, so one of the staffers brought in a blow dryer to see if we could do a little coaxing by heating the laminate. Nothing doing; it didn't heat the laminate to the 313° temperature that postforming manuals specify as the correct laminate bending temperature. So we got hold of a commercial heat gun at a local rental outlet. With it, we formed the laminate around radii down to about 1". We bent the laminate first, then applied contact cement.

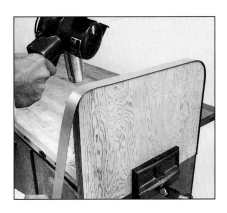

Wrapping a cylinder

Start by cutting the laminate to the length and width required. Be sure to allow extra for trimming. Apply contact cement to both mating surfaces, wait until the cement is dry to the touch, and apply the laminate to the substrate, except for the last 8 to 10". Slip a piece of waxed paper beneath the laminate, then carefully mark both edges of the laminate as shown.

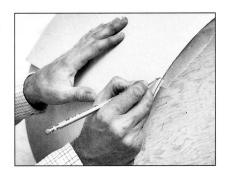

Carefully align one edge of a straightedge with the marks you just made, and clamp the straight-edge in place as shown. Run your router along the edge.

Picture-perfect joint lines

When you want a perfect joint line between two pieces of laminate that butt end-to-end or edge-to-edge, try this technique: Clamp two pieces of scrap to your workbench with a small space between them, then butt the two pieces of laminate together. Now secure the pieces of laminate with two more scrap lumber cleats. One pass with your router fitted with a carbide trimming bit, and you've got it made. Hold the router against one of the guides, and don't rotate the base of the router because many bases are not perfectly round.

Aligning geometric-patterned laminates

One of the new-generation "designer" laminates, the geometrics can cause you headaches if you're not careful. To make them look good, the surfaces you adhere them to must be square. This, combined with the fact that the patterns themselves aren't always true, makes aligning these

continued

PICTURE-PERFECT PARSONS TABLE
continued

laminates difficult. To make things easier on ourselves, we cut four like-sized wood scraps, and use them as shown. We make any needed adjustments, then apply contact cement to both of the surfaces and then lower the laminate down onto the substrate.

Hiding unsightly seam lines and defects

What if you end up with a less-than-perfect joint line or need to repair a defect of some sort? We decided to try a product called Kampel SEAMFIL from a local laminate retailer. We color-mixed some according to the directions and forced it into a seam. It worked as advertised, although we did have quite a time getting a color match. If we used the product again, we'd pay to have the factory color match the product for us so as to guarantee good results.

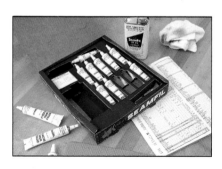

Finish-sanding wooden edge banding

When you choose the option of dressing up the edge of a shelf or counter with a wood banding, getting the wood perfectly flush

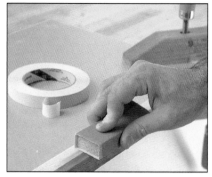

with the top of the laminate is tricky. When we apply the banding, we try to make sure the wood projects a bit above the laminate. Then we mask off the laminate and use a sanding block to bring the two surfaces flush. When we begin to see scuff marks on the masking tape, we call it quits.

Dressing up the edges of textured laminates

You can trim the edges of textured laminates as you do other laminates, but the bearing or pilot will follow all of the depressions and other irregularites in the material along the way. We dress the edge by working a triangular file carefully as shown here. A time-consuming technique to be sure, but necessary when working with these kinds of textured patterns.

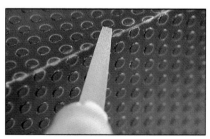

Three common countertop problems

Countertop installations give most people fits, mainly because the walls countertops fit up against are irregular. But scribing to fit allows you to compensate for those imperfections. In the instance shown at left, we used a thin piece of scrap material and a pencil to

scribe the irregularities of both walls onto the laminate.

Most laminate-trimming routers can't trim laminate right up to the wall. To trim the remainder of the excess material, we guide our scoring tool along a straightedge several times until we work our way through the material. Then we put the finishing touches on with a file.

Here's a tip for when you install a sink in a countertop. We mark the cutoff lines, then bore a ½" hole in each corner of the cutout. These holes do two things. First, they provide a radius at each inside corner, which helps to prevent stress cracking. And they also prevent you from accidentally scoring surrounding laminate. We score along each of the cutoff lines, then use a jigsaw with a metal-cutting blade to cut out the top (This blade reduces chip-out).

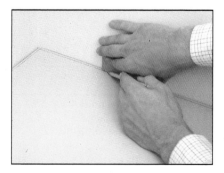

CHRISTMAS-TREE TRAY

Here's a new serving piece
you can craft in your
shop—and just in time for this
season's holiday entertaining.
The ¾"-deep cavity, easily
sculpted with your router, holds
plenty of tempting snacks or
candy for your guests.

**For routing ease, scrollsaw two
templates**

  1. Make three copies of the tree
pattern on *pages 60–61*. (We
photocopied ours.) Next, rip and
crosscut two 11×18" panels from
either ½"-thick plywood or
particleboard. Scribe a centerline
the long dimension on both panels.
Adhere one pattern copy to each
panel, aligning the centerlines and

the bottom. (We used spray
adhesive on the pattern backs.)

  2. Select one of the panels for
the Bottom template. Drill a
¼"-diameter start hole inside the
pattern line. Thread a scrollsaw
blade through the hole and cut out
the interior. Saw just wide of the
line, and then sand to the line to
make it as smooth as possible. (We
sanded the curved areas with a

continued

CHRISTMAS-TREE TRAY

continued

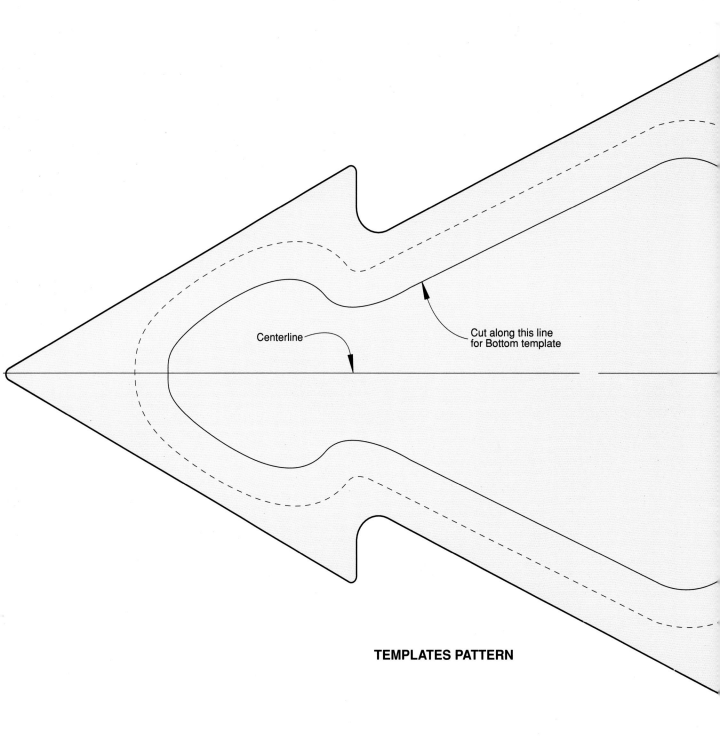

Centerline

Cut along this line
for Bottom template

TEMPLATES PATTERN

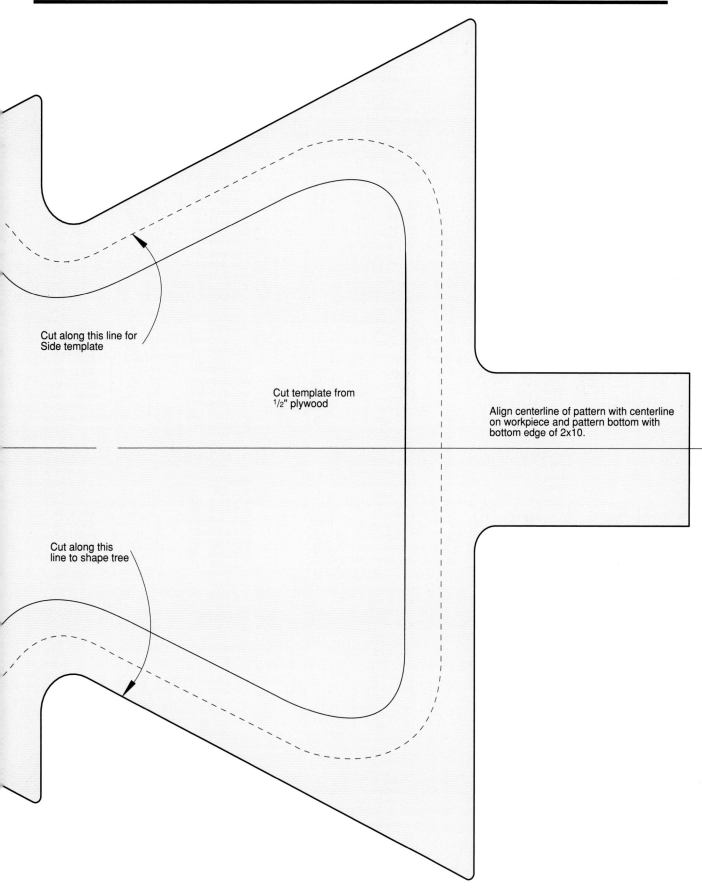

Cut along this line for
Side template

Cut template from
1/2" plywood

Align centerline of pattern with centerline
on workpiece and pattern bottom with
bottom edge of 2x10.

Cut along this
line to shape tree

continued

CHRISTMAS-TREE TRAY
continued

1"-diameter sanding drum mounted to our drill press.)

3. Make the remaining plywood panel your Side template. Scrollsaw it along the dashed line on the pattern. Sand to the cut line.

Note: *We sized the templates to work with the router bits and template guide bushings specified in the Buying Guide at far right. If you use bits or bushings of different size, you may need to change the opening size of the Side Template.*

The easy work lies ahead—just rout out the tree

1. Select a clear pine 2×10, and crosscut it to 18" long. Lightly scribe a centerline the length of the best face. Adhere your third pattern to the workpiece, aligning the centerlines and along the bottom.

2. Attach a ¾" O.D. guide bushing to your router's baseplate. (The center hole in the baseplate on our router accepts the Porter-Cable 1³⁄₁₆"-diameter threaded guide bushings. See the Buying Guide for a mail-order source for the guide bushings and special router bit. With some routers, you may have to purchase an adapter and modify the base to accept guide bushings). Next, chuck a "3-cuts-in-1" bit in your router. (See the Buying Guide for a mail-order source for the bit.)

3. Place the Bottom template on top of your workpiece, aligning the centerlines and the bottom. Nail the template to the 2×10. (We drove 4d finish nails at each corner.)

4. Place your router on the template, and set the bit to cut ⅛" deep. Now, rout the tray cavity as shown *right top*. When you reach final depth, pass the bit over the bottom several times to make it as uniformly flat as possible.

Tip: *To rout the cavity, make cuts at ⅛" or ¼" increments with a "3-cuts-in-1" router bit until you've cut ¾" deep. This bit cuts straight sides, and a smooth bottom to finish smoothing the routed surface.*

5. Replace the Bottom template with the Side template. Switch to a

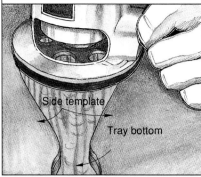

ROUTING THE BOTTOM OF THE TRAY

Side template

Tray bottom

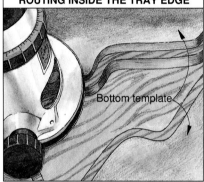

ROUTING INSIDE THE TRAY EDGE

Bottom template

1" O.D. guide bushing and a ¾" core-box bit on your router. Again, set the bit to cut ⅛" into your workpiece. Now, keeping the guide bushing against the edge of the template, rout around the edge of the tray as shown *above*. Increase bit cutting depth in small increments until the curvature at the bottom of the side edge meets the tray bottom.

Tip: *By switching to the Bottom Template a 1" O.D. bushing on your router base, and a ¾" corebox bit, you'll remove just enough stock from the side walls to form a gentle curve where the side meets the tray bottom.*

6. Remove the template. Scrape or sand out any unevenness in the routed bottom.

7. Scrollsaw or bandsaw around the outside pattern line to shape the tree. (We used a #9 scrollsaw blade with 11½ teeth per inch, but a ⅛" bandsaw blade with 14 teeth per inch also would work.) Sand the cut edge to the line, and then remove the pattern. Now, finish-

sand the entire tree with a 150-grit sandpaper.

8. Apply a non-toxic finish of your choice. (We applied three coats of White Lightning brand white stain and sealer to create a white pickle-stain effect. You can buy this product or similar ones at many craft stores.)

Supplies
2×10×18" pine, ½" plywood or particleboard for templates, finish.

Buying Guide
3-cuts-in-1 router bit. Carbide tipped, ¼" shank, ⁷⁄₁₆" diameter, cuts straight sides and flat bottom with ⅛"-radius corner. Catalog no. 555407. For current prices, contact Shopsmith, Inc., Attn: Order Dept., 3931 Image Dr., Dayton, OH 45414-2591. Credit-card orders telephone 800-543-7586.

Porter-cable template guide bushings. Sold individually or as a set. The ¾" O.D. bushing catalog no. 04133, 1" O.D. bushing catalog no. 04X32. Bushings require lock nut, catalog no. 04C44. Template guide kit model 42000 includes 7 different-sized bushings and two lock nuts. Catalog no. 04F52. For current prices, contact Woodcraft, P.O. Box 1686, Parkersburg, WV 26102-1686. Credit-card orders telephone 800-225-1153.

Project Tool List
Tablesaw
Scrollsaw
Drill press, ¼" bit
1" sanding drum
Router
    Guide bushings: ¾", 1"
    Bits: 3-cuts-in-1, ¾" core box
Finishing sander

Note: *We built the project using the tools listed. You may be able to substitute other tools or equipment for listed items you don't have. Additional common hand tools and clamps may be required to complete the project.*

TEA-FOR-TWO HUTCH

Home-hobbyist and woodworker Albert McCaffrey designed his first doll hutch for a granddaughter's Christmas gift a couple of years back. And with a little encouragement, he entered a second hutch in *Wood*® magazine's Build-A-Toy™ contest. Not surprisingly, his project became an instant hit with the judges.

Our toy hutch begins with basic carpentry

1. Select a ½X11¼X84" pine board and belt-sand both surfaces with 100-grit sandpaper. Using the Cutting diagram *below left* for reference, lay out the ½"-thick parts on the board. Now, rip and crosscut two sides (A), one bottom (B), one countertop (C), two ends (D), two shelves (E), and one crown (F) to dimensions listed on the Bill of Materials on *page 64*. You may edge-glue narrower stock for the wide parts such as the countertop, sides, and bottom.

2. Mount a ¼" dado on your tablesaw, and cut a ¼"-deep rabbet along one long edge on both sides (A). With the same saw setting, rabbet one edge of both end pieces (D), stopping the cut 1⅛" from the top on each end as shown on the Upper Cabinet Side View drawing on *page 66*. Square the ends of these rabbets with a chisel. Now, using double-faced tape, stack the two end pieces face-to-face with the rabbeted edges together.

3. Make full-sized copies of all patterns on *page 67*. To make a full-sized End pattern from the gridded pattern, first join sheets of paper to form a rectangle about 1" larger than the part. Starting at one corner, scribe 1" squares across the paper. Next, using the gridded patterns as your guide, plot the points where the pattern outline crosses the grid lines. Now, draw a line connecting these points. (We *continued*

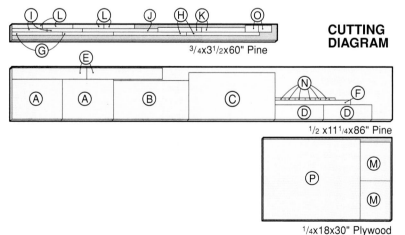

CUTTING DIAGRAM

¾x3½x60" Pine

½ x11¼x86" Pine

¼x18x30" Plywood

TEA-FOR-TWO HUTCH
continued

Bill of Materials

Part	T	W	L	Mat.	Qty.
A side	½"	8¾"	11½"	P	2
B bottom	½"	8½"	17"	P	1
C countertop	½"	10¼"	19½"	P	1
D end	½"	3¼"	10⅞"	P	2
E shelf	½"	2½"	17"	P	2
F crown	½"	1"	17"	P	1
G stile	¾"	¾"	11½"	P	2
H rail	¾"	¾"	16½"	P	2
I cleat	¾"	¾"	8"	P	2
J spanner	¾"	½"	17"	P	1
K door stile	¾"	1"	9⅞"	P	4
L door rail	¾"	1"	6 15/16"	P	4
M panel	¼"	6⅞"	8½"	PW	2
N feet	½"	¾"	2¼"	P	6
O stop	1½"	1"	3"	P	1
P* back	¼"	17⅝"	21¾"	PW	1

*Cut part marked with an * to size during construction. Please read the instructions before cutting.

Material Key: P—pine; PW—plywood
Supplies: 4d finish nails, ¾"X16 brads, # 6X1" flathead wood screws, 4–1X1" brass hinges (Stanley 80-3200), 2–¾" door pulls, finish.

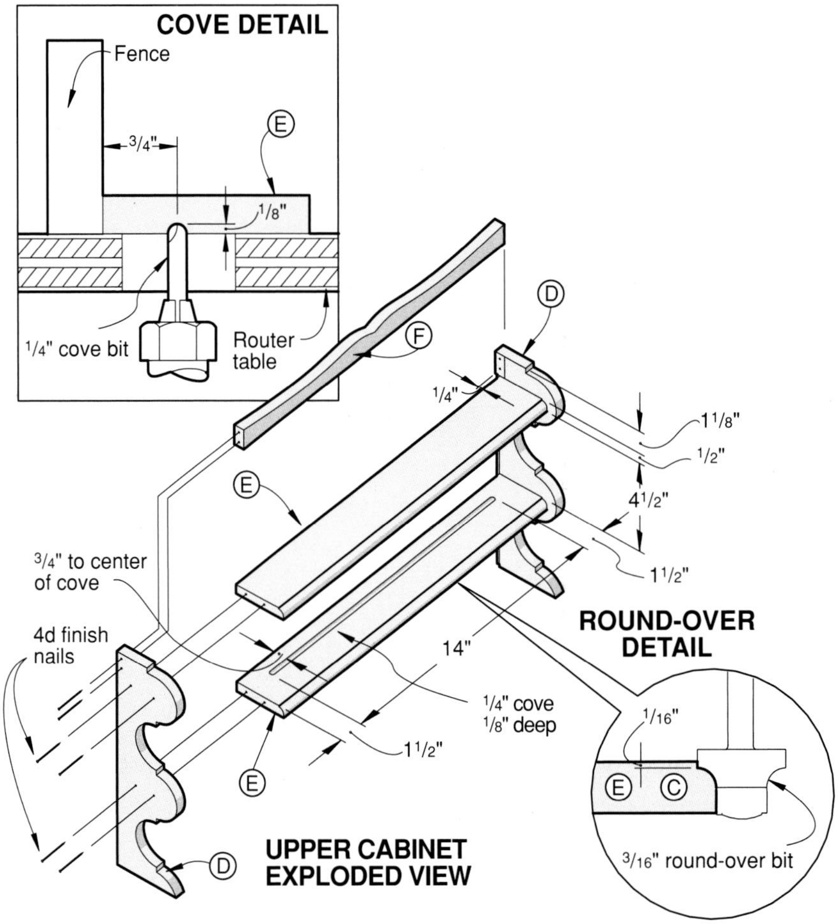
COVE DETAIL
Fence
3/4"
E
1/8"
1/4" cove bit
Router table
F
D
1/4"
1 1/8"
1/2"
4 1/2"
1 1/2"
E
3/4" to center of cove
4d finish nails
14"
ROUND-OVER DETAIL
1/4" cove
1/8" deep
1 1/2"
1/16"
E C
E
3/16" round-over bit
D
UPPER CABINET EXPLODED VIEW

used french curves to draw the curves of the pattern.) If you prefer to enlarge the gridded patterns on an enlarging copier, set the enlargement at the percentage stated on the pattern.

4. Adhere your full-sized End pattern to an end blank, aligning the back edges of the pattern and piece. Scrollsaw the parts to shape, cutting just outside the line. Next, sand the cut edges to the line, remove the pattern, and separate the pieces. (We used a 2"-diameter sanding drum to sand the curved edges, and hand-sanded the remaining edges.)

5. Tape your two copies of the full-sized Crown half-pattern together where instructed to join, and then adhere it to the crown blank. Now, saw the crown (F) trim piece to shape, and then sand the sawed edges.

6. Chuck a piloted 3/16" round-over bit into your table-mounted router, and set it to cut as shown on the Round-Over detail *above right*. With it, rout one edge on both shelves, and along the top front and side edges on the countertop. Switch to a ¼" cove bit, and set it up as shown on the Cove detail *above*. With it, rout a blind groove in the counter-top and one shelf where dimen-sioned on the Upper Cabinet Exploded View drawing *above* and the Exploded View drawing *opposite*. (We clamped a fence and stopblocks to the router table to control groove position and length.)

***Tip:** If you wish to add a shelf inside the cabinet, cut it to the same length as the bottom, and as wide as you want it to be. Then, nail through the sides to hold it in place.*

7. From ¾"-thick pine, cut two ¾X11½" stiles (G) and two ¾X16½" rails (H) for the cabinet face frame. Cut two ¾X8" cleats (I), and one ½X17" spanner (J) from the same stock. Next, drill 9/64" shank holes through the cleats where shown on the Exploded View drawing. Now, glue and screw the cleats to the cabinet sides, aligning them along the top and front edges of the sides where shown.

Next, begin assembling the cabinet and doors

1. Dry-assemble the face frame, cabinet sides, bottom, and spanner. (We used bar clamps to hold the parts together temporarily.) Place

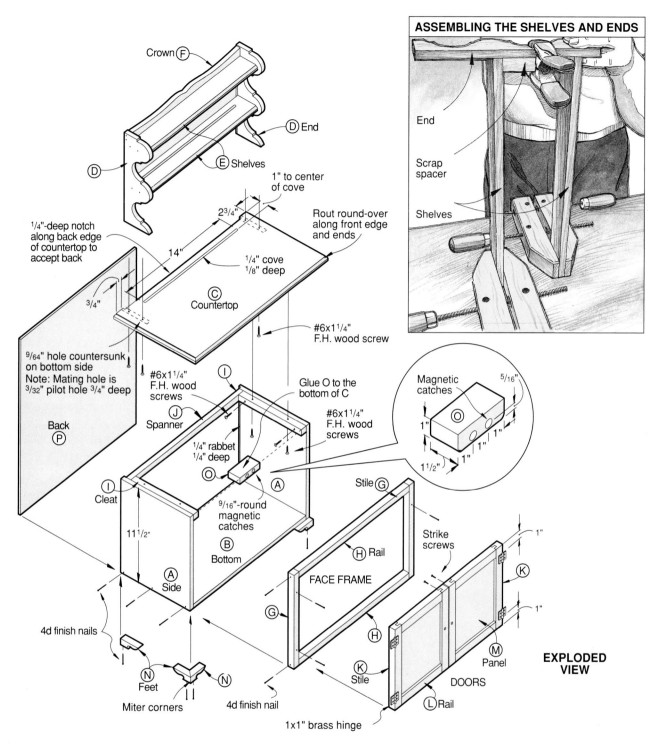

ASSEMBLING THE SHELVES AND ENDS

Crown (F)

(D) End

(D)

(E) Shelves

(D)

End

Scrap
spacer

Shelves

1" to center
of cove

2³/₄"

Rout round-over
along front edge
and ends

¹/₄"-deep notch
along back edge
of countertop to
accept back

14"

¹/₄" cove
¹/₈" deep

(C)
Countertop

³/₄"

⁹/₆₄" hole countersunk
on bottom side
Note: Mating hole is
³/₃₂" pilot hole ³/₄" deep

Back
(P)

#6x1¹/₄"
F.H. wood
screws

(I)

(J)

Spanner

Glue O to the
bottom of C

#6x1¹/₄"
F.H. wood screw

#6x1¹/₄"
F.H. wood
screws

Magnetic
catches

⁵/₁₆"

(O)

1"

1"

1"

1¹/₂"

1"

¹/₄" rabbet
¹/₄" deep

(O)

(A)

Stile (G)

(I)
Cleat

⁹/₁₆"-round
magnetic
catches

Strike
screws

1"

(K)

11¹/₂"

(B)
Bottom

(H) Rail

FACE FRAME

(A)
Side

(G)

(H)

1"

(M)
Panel

EXPLODED
VIEW

4d finish nails

(N)
Feet

(N)

Miter corners

4d finish nail

1x1" brass hinge

(K)
Stile

DOORS

(L) Rail

the face frame on the cabinet front to check fit. Adjust the part dimensions if necessary. Glue, nail, and square the face frame. Next, glue and nail the cabinet sides to the cabinet bottom. Square the cabinet, and then glue and nail the spanner in place. Now, nail and glue the face frame to the cabinet front.

Tip: To prevent the nails from splitting the wood when assembling the cabinet, cut the head off a 4d finish nail, and chuck it into your electric drill. Then, use it to pilot the nail holes before you drive the nails.

2. Using the dimensions found on the Upper Cabinet Exploded View drawing *opposite*, glue and

nail together the shelves, ends, and crown, squaring the parts as you work. (We cut a 4¹/₂"-long scrap, and placed it as shown *above* to space the shelves while assembling the top. We also used a ¹/₄"-thick scrap to inset the two shelves ¹/₄" in from the back edge of the ends.)
continued

TEA-FOR-TWO HUTCH
continued

FITTING THE HUTCH DOORS

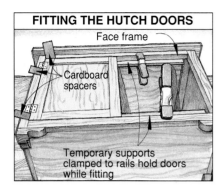

Face frame

Cardboard spacers

Temporary supports clamped to rails hold doors while fitting

SCROLLSAWING THE FOOT

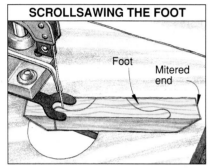

Foot

Mitered end

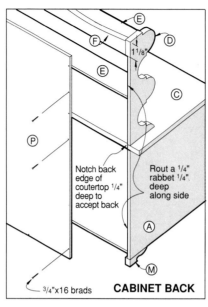

Notch back edge of countertop 1/4" deep to accept back

Rout a 1/4" rabbet 1/4" deep along side

1 1/8"

3/4"x16 brads

CABINET BACK

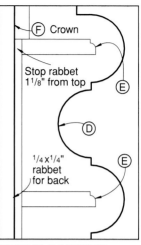

Crown

Stop rabbet 1 1/8" from top

1/4 x 1/4" rabbet for back

UPPER CABINET
(SIDE VIEW)

Note on the Upper Cabinet Side View drawing at *far right*, how the bottom edge of the crown aligns with the ends rabbets.

3. For the doors, cut four stiles (K) and rails (L) to dimension. Using a 1/4" dado set, cut a 1/4"-wide groove centered along one edge of each rail and stile as shown on the Groove detail on *page 67*. Next, lay the rails on their sides, and form the tenons on each end as shown on the Tenon detail on *page 67*. (We tested our saw setting by first cutting scrap and test-fitting the trial tenons in the grooves. We then adjusted the saw, verified the new setting, and cut the tenons on the rail ends.) Dry-assemble one door frame, measure the opening, and cut two door panels (M) to that size. Finish-sand all door parts. Now, glue, assemble, clamp, and square both doors. Do not glue the plywood panels in the grooves.

4. Trim the doors, and then fit them into the face-frame opening. (As shown *above top*, we clamped scrap bars inside the cabinet to hold the doors within the face frame. When trimming, we removed equal

amounts of material from each side on both doors. Also, note that we used thin-cardboard strips to evenly space the doors.) Next, attach the hinges to the frame, mark the centerpoints for the hinge screw holes on the door, drill the pilot holes, and then drive the screws. Remove the hinges. Locate and drill the holes for your doorknob screws.

5. Make the cabinet feet (N) by first cutting a piece of 1/2"-thick pine to 3/4x15". Next, using the full-sized Foot pattern, trace the outline of six feet onto the piece. (As shown *above left*, we miter-cut the corners first, then scrollsawed the feet [N] to shape.) Sand the sawed edges. Now, glue and nail the feet to the cabinet bottom where shown on the Exploded View drawing on *page 65*.

6. Place the countertop on the cabinet, align the back edge, and center it from side to side. Next, place the upper cabinet on the countertop, and align the back edges. Temporarily clamp this assembly. Place your try square in the back rabbets. Now, using it as a straightedge, scribe lines across the countertop's back edge marking the limits for the 1/4"- deep back notch. See the Cabinet Back drawing *above*.

7. Cut the notch for the back into the countertop, starting and stopping at the lines you just made. (We

made this blind-rip cut on our tablesaw by locking the fence 10" from the inside of the blade. We placed the top's front edge against the fence, and carefully lowered it over the saw blade, starting and stopping the cut 1 1/2" from the marks. We finished the cut with our jigsaw.) Next, locate, mark, and drill the 9/64" shank holes in the countertop. Now, attach the countertop to the upper cabinet assembly with #6x1 1/4" flathead wood screws.

8. Attach the countertop to the cabinet by driving the #6x1" screws through the predrilled holes in the cleats and into the top. Make the door stop (O) by gluing two 3/4"-thick pieces face-to-face. Drill the holes as detailed on the Exploded View drawing. Next, insert the round magnetic catches in the holes, letting them extend 1/16". Center and glue the stop under the countertop and against the face frame.

9. Measure the back opening and cut a 1/4" plywood panel (P) to fit. Do not attach it yet.

You're nearly finished: Get out the play dishes

1. Set all nails and fill the holes. Finish-sand all parts and joints with a 150-grit sandpaper.

2. Apply the finish of your choice. (We removed the countertop, and applied two coats of polyurethane to it. We brushed-

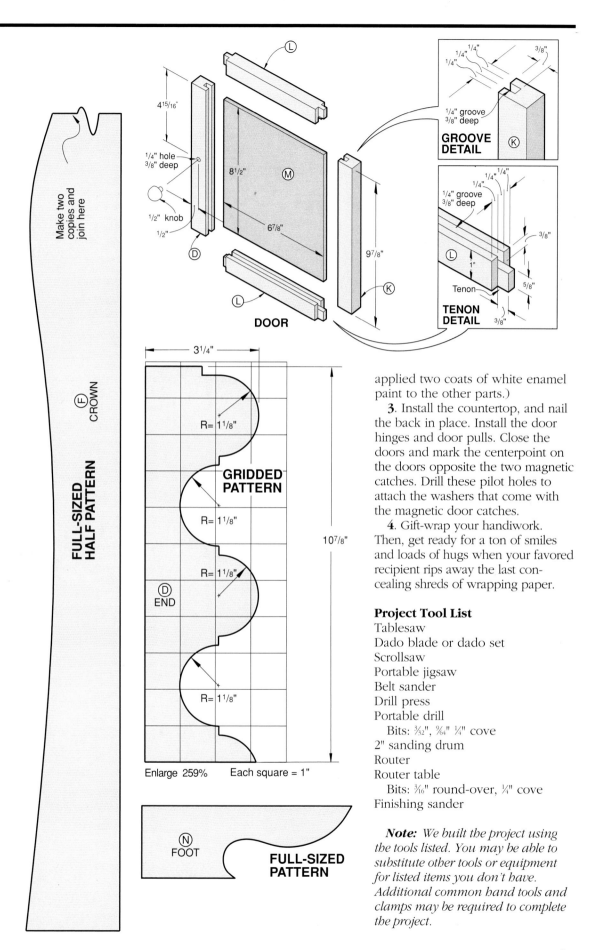

GROOVE DETAIL

1/4" groove
3/8" deep

Ⓚ

1/4"
1/4"
1/4"
3/8"

TENON DETAIL

1/4" groove
3/8" deep

1/4"
1/4"
1/4"

3/8"

Ⓛ

1"

Tenon

5/8"

3/8"

Ⓛ

4¹⁵/₁₆"

1/4" hole
3/8" deep

1/2" knob

1/2"

Ⓓ

8¹/₂"

Ⓜ

6⁷/₈"

9⁷/₈"

Ⓚ

Ⓛ

DOOR

Make two copies and join here

Ⓕ
CROWN

FULL-SIZED HALF PATTERN

3¹/₄"

R= 1¹/₈"

GRIDDED PATTERN

R= 1¹/₈"

R= 1¹/₈"

Ⓓ
END

R= 1¹/₈"

10⁷/₈"

Enlarge 259%   Each square = 1"

Ⓝ
FOOT

FULL-SIZED PATTERN

applied two coats of white enamel paint to the other parts.)

3. Install the countertop, and nail the back in place. Install the door hinges and door pulls. Close the doors and mark the centerpoint on the doors opposite the two magnetic catches. Drill these pilot holes to attach the washers that come with the magnetic door catches.

4. Gift-wrap your handiwork. Then, get ready for a ton of smiles and loads of hugs when your favored recipient rips away the last concealing shreds of wrapping paper.

Project Tool List
Tablesaw
Dado blade or dado set
Scrollsaw
Portable jigsaw
Belt sander
Drill press
Portable drill
    Bits: ³/₃₂", ⁵/₆₄" ¹/₄" cove
2" sanding drum
Router
Router table
    Bits: ³/₁₆" round-over, ¹/₄" cove
Finishing sander

Note: *We built the project using the tools listed. You may be able to substitute other tools or equipment for listed items you don't have. Additional common hand tools and clamps may be required to complete the project.*

MANCALA MARBLE GAME

Introduce an ancient game to the latest generation of kids by making this intriguing project. Mancala comes to us from Africa and southern Asia and was originally played with shells or pebbles in pockets scooped out of the earth. Our version features a striped walnut and maple laminated board with routed pockets. We even tell you how to play.

Laminate the board

1. From 1¹⁵⁄₁₆"-thick (6/4) stock (we used maple), rip and crosscut one piece to 2¼×27" (A), and two pieces to 1⁷⁄₁₆×27" (B). Now, rip and crosscut four pieces to ¼×27" (C). (See the Cutting diagram, the Assembly drawing, and the End detail *opposite*.)

Note: *If you don't have 1¹⁵⁄₁₆"-thick stock available, you can laminate two pieces of ¾"-thick stock together face-to-face, and then plane or resaw it to the actual thickness needed.*

2. To make the decorative ⅛"-wide walnut strips (D), rip and crosscut two ¾"-thick pieces to 1⁵⁄₁₆×27". Next, set the fence on your tablesaw ⅛" from the inside of the saw blade. Now, resaw six ⅛"-thick strips from the two walnut pieces.

3. Assemble pieces A, B, C, and D in the order shown on the End detail and the Assembly drawing. Next, apply glue (we used white woodworker's glue) to the adjoining surfaces, assemble the pieces on a length of waxed paper, and clamp the board as shown *below*. (We placed scrap strips between the clamps and the edges of the lamination to prevent marring. We then clamped wood strips crosswise [sandwiching waxed paper between the cross strips and the lamination] on the top and bottom of the lamination to even the surfaces while the glue set.) Wipe off any glue squeezeout. If you find it difficult to

glue a lamination with this many pieces, assemble the left and right thirds (B, C, D) separately.

Next, prepare the router template

1. Rip and crosscut one piece of ¼" hardboard or plywood to 6⅞×26". Using the dimensions on the Router Template drawing on *page 71,* carefully lay out and mark all of the hole and screw centerpoints onto the face of the hardboard.

2. Drill, and then countersink the four ⅛"-screw holes in each corner of the hardboard where marked.

3. Chuck a circle cutter in your drill-press, and clamp a large piece of scrap to the drill press table. Next, clamp a fence to the scrap table top 1⅛" from the center of the circle cutter's pilot bit. Now, adjust the circle cutter's arm to cut a 1⁷⁄₁₆"-radius (2⅞"-diameter) circle.

4. Place one edge of the hardboard against the fence, and align the centerpoint of one of the large inside circles under the pilot bit. Clamp the hardboard securely to the drill press table, and cut the circle. Repeat the procedure to cut the other 11 inside circles in the hardboard as shown *opposite bottom*.

5. To cut the circles for the elongated openings at the ends, reset your circle cutter to cut a 1³⁄₁₆"-radius (2⅜"-diameter) circle. Move the fence 1⅛" from the pilot

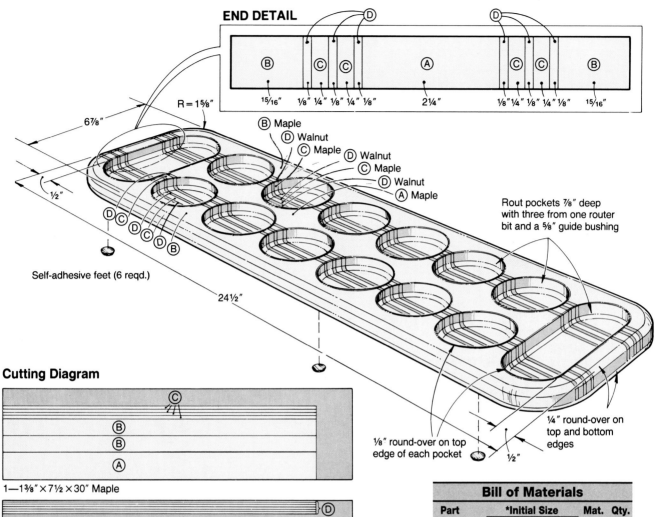

END DETAIL

Ⓓ   Ⓓ   Ⓓ

Ⓑ   Ⓒ   Ⓒ   Ⓐ   Ⓒ   Ⓒ   Ⓑ

¹⁵⁄₁₆″   ¹⁄₈″ ¹⁄₄″ ¹⁄₈″ ¹⁄₄″ ¹⁄₈″   2¹⁄₄″   ¹⁄₈″ ¹⁄₄″ ¹⁄₈″ ¹⁄₄″ ¹⁄₈″   ¹⁵⁄₁₆″

R = 1⁵⁄₈″

6⁷⁄₈″

¹⁄₂″

Ⓑ Maple
Ⓓ Walnut
Ⓒ Maple   Ⓓ Walnut
Ⓒ Maple
Ⓓ Walnut
Ⓐ Maple

Self-adhesive feet (6 reqd.)

Ⓓ Ⓒ Ⓓ Ⓒ Ⓓ Ⓑ

24¹⁄₂″

Rout pockets ⁷⁄₈″ deep
with three from one router
bit and a ⁵⁄₈″ guide bushing

¹⁄₈″ round-over on top
edge of each pocket

¹⁄₄″ round-over on
top and bottom
edges

¹⁄₂″

Cutting Diagram

Ⓒ

Ⓑ

Ⓑ

Ⓐ

1—1³⁄₈″ × 7¹⁄₂ × 30″ Maple

Ⓓ

1—³⁄₄ × 3¹⁄₂ × 30″ Walnut

Bill of Materials

Part	*Initial Size			Mat.	Qty.
	T	W	L		
A	1⁵⁄₁₆″	2¹⁄₄″	27″	M	1
B	1⁵⁄₁₆″	1⁷⁄₁₆″	27″	M	2
C	1⁵⁄₁₆″	¹⁄₄″	27″	M	4
D	¹⁄₈″	1³⁄₈″	27″	W	6

*All parts in the lamination are cut larger
intially, and then trimmed to finished size.
Please read the instructions before cutting.

Material Key: M—maple, W—walnut
Supplies: 4–#4×¹⁄₂″ flathead wood screws,
¹⁄₄″ hardboard, white woodworker's glue,
6–self-adhesive feet

Size the board and rout the pockets

1. Remove the clamps from the laminated board. Scrape or sand off any glue squeeze-out. Now, plane or sand the board to 1¹⁄₄″ thickness, and crosscut it to 26″ long.

2. Place strips of double-faced tape on the underside of the template. Next, place the template on the top surface of the board, *continued*

bit's centerpoint. Now, cut the four end circles where indicated by the centerpoints. Finally, use a scrollsaw to saw away the material between the paired circles, and sand the cutlines straight. (We sanded ours with a 1″-diameter drum sander mounted to the drill press.)

MANCALA MARBLE GAME
continued

carefully aligning the edges and ends of the template with those on the lamination. Drill ¹⁄₁₆" pilot holes ⅜" deep into the board for the four corner screws. Now, screw the template to the laminated board with #4x½" flathead wood screws. The screw holes in the board will be cut off when you round the corners later.

3. Mount a ⅝" guide bushing on your router and chuck a 3 from 1 bit in the collet. (See the Buying Guide for a mail-order source.) Set the bit to cut ⅛" deep, and start routing the 14 pockets in the board as shown *opposite top.* (We clamped the board to our benchtop to keep it from moving while routing.) Increase the router's cutting depth in ⅛" increments until you have cut all pockets ⅞" deep as shown in the Routing Detail drawing *opposite.* During the last cutting pass, thoroughly clean the bottom of each pocket to form a smooth, level bottom. Remove the template when finished.

4. Trim the lamination to 24½" long by crosscutting ¾" from each end of the board. Once you've squared the board, turn it over and scribe a 1⅝" radius on each corner. Using a bandsaw, cut the corners to shape, and sand. (We sawed just outside the line, and then sanded to the line using our disc sander.)

5. Remove the ⅝" guide bushing and the bit from your router, and chuck a ¼" round-over bit in the collet. Round over the edges of the board. Now, switch to a ⅛" roundover bit and carefully round over the edges of the pockets. If you don't have a ⅛" round-over bit, use the ¼" bit.

6. Finish-sand the game board. Apply the finish of your choice. (We sprayed on three coats of varnish, sanding lightly between coats.)

7. After the finish has dried, adhere six self-adhesive rubber feet (available at most homecenters) to the bottom of the game board. Add the marbles (available at toy and game stores). Now, find an opponent for your first game.

How to play mancala

There are many ways to play mancala. We'll describe a simple version. We also suggest you research and try other interesting or more challenging versions of this game, too.

Preparing the board

To play, you need an opponent, the board, and 72 marbles, seeds, or shells. Place the board between you and your opponent. Now, looking at the game board, the six pockets along the front belong to you, and the elongated pocket at your right serves as your treasury. The six pockets on the opposite side and remaining treasury pocket belong to your opponent. (See *right.*) To start, place six marbles in each round pocket. Your objective: to accumulate more marbles in your treasury than your opponent collects. In one version, play continues until the winner collects all of the marbles.

Playing the game

The starting player (player one) picks up all of the marbles in any one of the pockets on his

or her side of the board. Moving counterclockwise, player one drops a marble in each pocket (opponent's too), including his or her treasury, but not in the opponent's treasury. After dropping the last marble, this player gathers up the marbles in that pocket and continues play until he or she drops the last marble in hand into an empty pocket. At that point, player two starts play from his or her side. If a player's last marble drops into his or her treasury, that player continues from any of the pockets on his or her side. The game ends when all marbles have been deposited in the two treasuries.

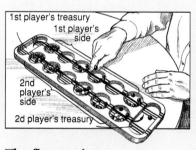

1st player's treasury
1st player's side
2nd player's side
2d player's treasury

The finer points

Playing strategies should become obvious as you gain experience. For example, when starting a turn, it usually works best to start at the pocket with the largest number of marbles. When possible, count ahead so that your last marble in hand goes into your treasury. Also, select a starting pocket containing enough marbles to allow you to avoid ending in an empty pocket, which will end your turn.

Buying Guide
• **3 from 1 router bit.** ¼" shaft, catalog no. 06V22. For current prices, contact Woodcraft, 41 Atlantic Ave., P.O. Box 4000, Woburn, MA 01888. Phone: 800-225-1153.

• **Router guide bushing set.** Includes a universal router base plate; ⁵⁄₁₆", ⁷⁄₁₆" short and long lengths; and a ⅝"-diameter bushing. Catalog no. 11V12. For current prices, contact Woodcraft, address at *left.*

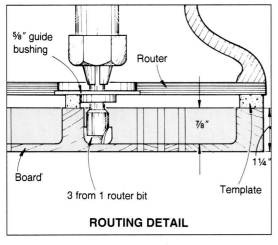

⁵⁄₈" guide bushing

Router

Board

3 from 1 router bit

⁷⁄₈"

1¼"

Template

ROUTING DETAIL

Project Tool List

Tablesaw
Scrollsaw
Bandsaw
Drill press
  ⅛" bit
  Circle cutter
  1" drum sander
Router
  Bits: 3 from 1, ⅛" round-over,
    ¼" round-over
  Guide bushing: ⅝"
Finish sander

Note: *We built the project using the tools listed. You may be able to substitute other tools or equipment for listed items you don't have. Additional common hand tools and clamps may be required to complete the project.*

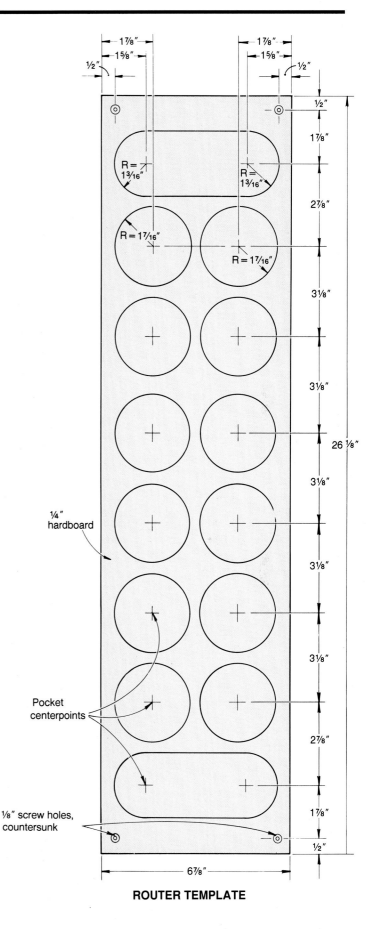

ROUTER TEMPLATE

RESPLENDENT PENDANT

More than just jewelry, our tasteful timepiece not only tells the hour and minute of the day, but it also shows the date and phases of the moon. A cinch to make, the pendant will remind the lucky recipient of both your affection and your woodworking skills.

Plane or resaw a piece of stock (we used maple), that measures at least 2¼" wide by 12" long to ½" thick. (We used a 12"-long piece for safety when machining.)

Mark a centerpoint 2" from one end of the stock. With a compass, mark a 1¾"-diameter circle (⅞" radius) locating the compass point on the centerpoint. Chuck a 1⅜" Forstner bit into your drill press. Center the bit directly over the

marked centerpoint and clamp the stock to your drill-press table. Drill a ¼"-deep hole.

With a bandsaw or scrollsaw, cut just outside the marked line and then sand to the line (we used our disc sander). Cut a piece of 1"-diameter dowel to 12" long. Using hotmelt adhesive, adhere one end of the dowel to the back of the pendant. Fit your table-mounted router with a ³⁄₁₆" round-

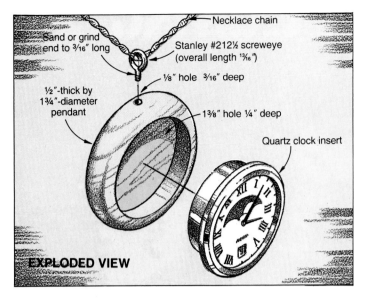

Necklace chain

Sand or grind end to ³⁄₁₆" long

Stanley #212½ screweye (overall length ¹³⁄₁₆")

⅛" hole ³⁄₁₆" deep

½"-thick by 1¾"-diameter pendant

1⅜" hole ¼" deep

Quartz clock insert

EXPLODED VIEW

FULL-SIZED BEAD DETAIL

Bead

³⁄₁₆" round-over

³⁄₁₆" round-over bit

¹⁄₁₆"

For better control and to keep your fingers safely away from the bit when routing such a small piece, adhere a dowel to the pendant blank.

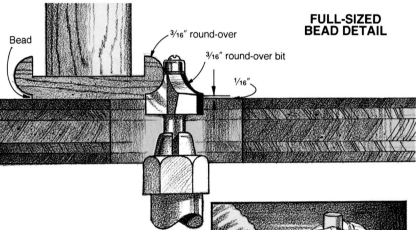

Separate the pendant and dowel, and scrape off the hotmelt. Hand-sand the pendant smooth. Grind the threaded end of a Stanley #212½ brass screw eye to ³⁄₁₆" long. Rub the brass with 0000 steel wool to polish the finish. Epoxy the end of the screw eye into the ⅛" hole in the pendant. Add the finish to the pendant. Loop a necklace (we used a 24" gold French rope) through the screw eye. Slide the friction-fit clock insert into position.

Buying Guide
- **Mini-quartz clock insert.**

Shows date, time, and moon phase, product no. 15063N. For current prices, contact Klockit, P.O. Box 636. Lake Geneva, WI 53147. Or, call 800-556-2548 to order.

Project Tool List
Tablesaw
Bandsaw or scrollsaw
Drill press
  Bits: ⅛", 1⅜"
Disc sander
Router
  Router table
  ³⁄₁₆" round-over bit

Note: *We built the project using the tools listed. You may be able to substitute other tools or equipment for listed items you don't have. Additional common hand tools and clamps may be required to complete the project.*

over bit and a fence. As shown in the drawing *above,* rout a ³⁄₁₆" round-over along the front edge of the pendant.

Remove the dowel from the back of the pendant, and use a chisel to scrape off the hotmelt adhesive. Adhere one end of the dowel in the pendant hole. Using the same bit, rout a bead on the back of the pendant to the size shown on the Bead detail *above.*

With the pendant still attached to the dowel, drill a ⅛" hole ³⁄₁₆" deep into the pendant where shown in the drawing *top left.*

STYLIZED MEAT CARVING BOARD

Carve your next holiday turkey or roast in style on this unique carving board. The maple lamination will withstand years of hard use, and the routed juice groove will catch those messy but oh-so-tasty drippings.

Note: *Unless you own a pin router, you'll need to build the Delta-Wing Pin Routing Attachment described on pages 75–77 to rout the pattern in the carving board. For more information about how to use the pin routing attachment and how to make the templates, see "Template Routing" starting on page 32.*

First make the maple lamination

1. Cut 16 pieces of ¾" maple to 1⅜" wide by 19" long.

2. Glue and clamp the pieces together *face to face,* keeping the edges flush. (We clamped scrap stock across the pieces to keep them flat.)

3. Plane or belt-sand the top and bottom surfaces, being careful to keep the board flat. (We continually checked the surface for depressions with a straightedge.) The extra thickness allows up to ⅛" for scraping and sanding.

4. Cut the maple lamination to finished size (12x18"). (Our original maple stock was a fraction over ¾" thick, so we had to trim the lamination to a 12" width. If your lamination measures wider than 12", trim equal amounts off both sides instead of taking it all off one edge.)

5. Lay out a 1½" radius at each corner, then with a bandsaw, cut the corners to shape. Sand the four rounded corners smooth.

6. Using the Handle detail *opposite, bottom,* as a guide, rout a ¾" cove ⅝" deep 5¼" long centered along each end of the lamination.

The template comes next

1. Cut a piece of ¼" plywood for the template and a piece of ¾" plywood for the carrier board to 12x18".

Note: *Take your time when laying out the pattern, cutting and sanding the pieces, and nailing them to the carrier board. The quality of the routed pattern depends on the careful preparation of the template pieces.*

2. Transfer the template to the ¼" plywood, using the dimensions on the Template drawing *opposite, top,* as a guide.

3. Cut the template pieces (except the straight ⅜"-wide strips forming the outer border) to shape using a scrollsaw or a bandsaw. From ¼" plywood, cut the border strips to size on a tablesaw, so the grain runs lengthwise on each strip.

4. Sand all template pieces to finished shape. Now, glue and nail the pieces to the ¾" plywood carrier board to form the template, carefully keeping the grooves at least ⅜" wide. (We used the ⅜" guide pin from the pin routing attachment as a spacer to maintain the ⅜" gap between the pieces.)

5. Rip a long piece of ¾" scrap to a 1" width, and then crosscut it to 20" long. Now, cut eight pieces 1½" long from the length for the positioner blocks. Drill shank and pilot holes and mount two blocks to each edge of the carrier board with wood screws where shown on the drawing. Then, secure the carrier board to the maple lamination with double-faced tape. The blocks and tape help hold the lamination firmly against the carrier board when routing.

Ready, set, rout

1. Prepare the pin routing attachment for routing as explained on *page 36* under the

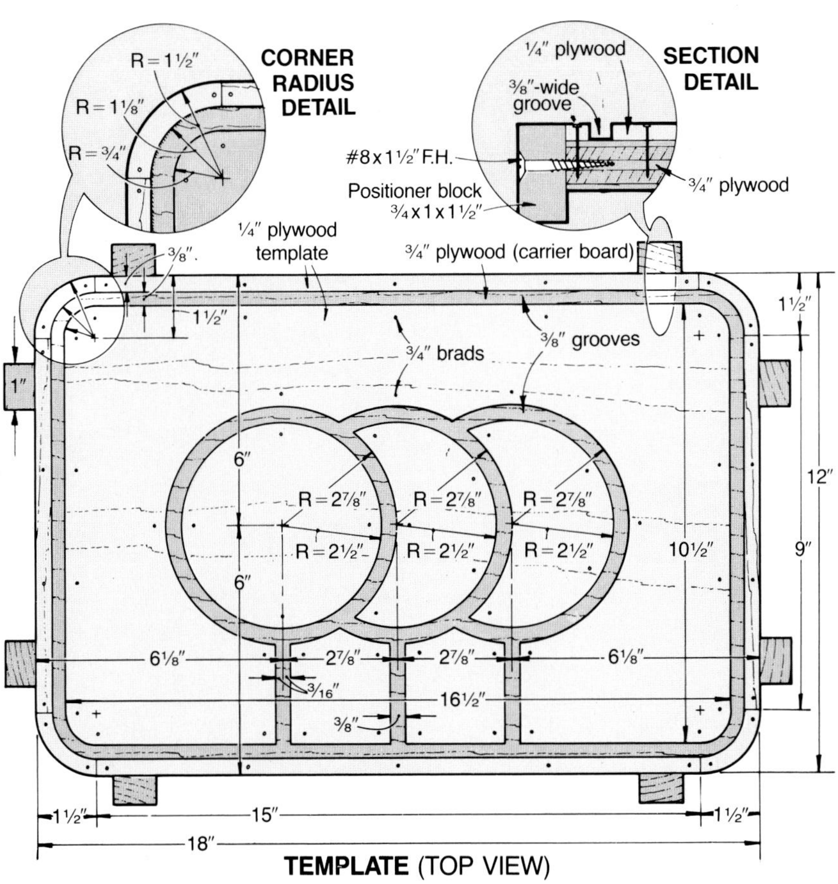
CORNER RADIUS DETAIL
R=1½″
R=1⅛″
R=¾″
SECTION DETAIL
¼″ plywood
⅜″-wide groove
#8x1½″ F.H.
Positioner block ¾x1x1½″
¾″ plywood
¼″ plywood template
¾″ plywood (carrier board)
⅜″
1½″
¾″ brads
⅜″ grooves
1″
6″
6″
R=2⅞″
R=2⅞″
R=2⅞″
R=2½″
R=2½″
R=2½″
10½″
12″
9″
6⅛″
2⅞″
2⅞″
6⅛″
3⁄16″
16½″
⅜″
1½″
15″
1½″
18″

TEMPLATE (TOP VIEW)

head "Routing Your Project—The Pin Router Method."

2. Chuck a ⅜" core box bit (also called a round nose) to your table-mounted router so the top of the bit extends ⅜" above the router table.

3. With the router turned off, position the lamination/template assembly with the ⅜" guide pin *in* one of the grooves in the template, ⅛" above the top of the router bit.

4. Firmly holding the lamination with one hand, start the router, lower the lamination onto the spinning bit, and lock the pin router arm down with the hold-down. Now, slowly and steadily move the lamination so the guide pin follows the pattern. Make the pin contact both sides of each groove, *one side at a time.* Doing this ensures recesses with accurately cut side walls.

5. When you've completed routing the pattern, turn off the router, wait for the bit to quit spinning, and then unlock the arm. After checking to see that the bit made all cuts to your satisfaction, separate the work from the carrier board. Finally, finish-sand the carving board, including the juice groove. Apply a nontoxic finish. (We used Behlen's salad bowl finish.)

Project Tools List

Tablesaw
Bandsaw
Belt sander
Portable drill
Router
  Router table with pin routing jig
  Bits: ¾" cove, ⅜" core box
Finishing sander

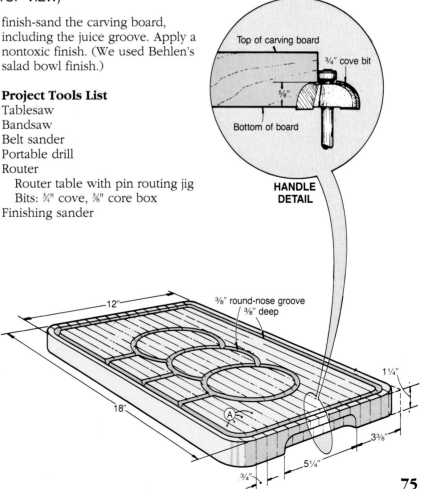

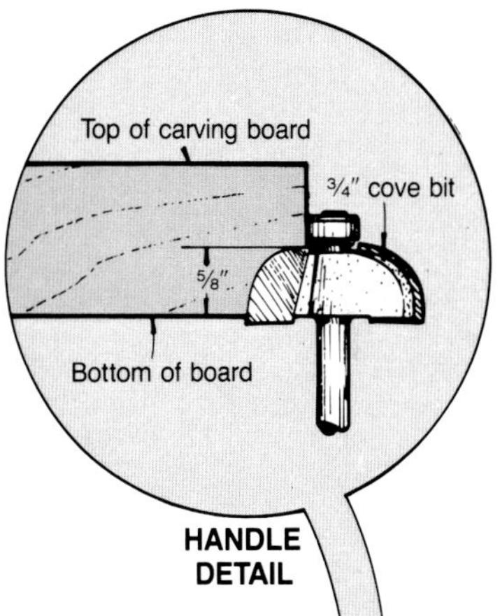
Top of carving board
¾″ cove bit
⅝″
Bottom of board
HANDLE DETAIL

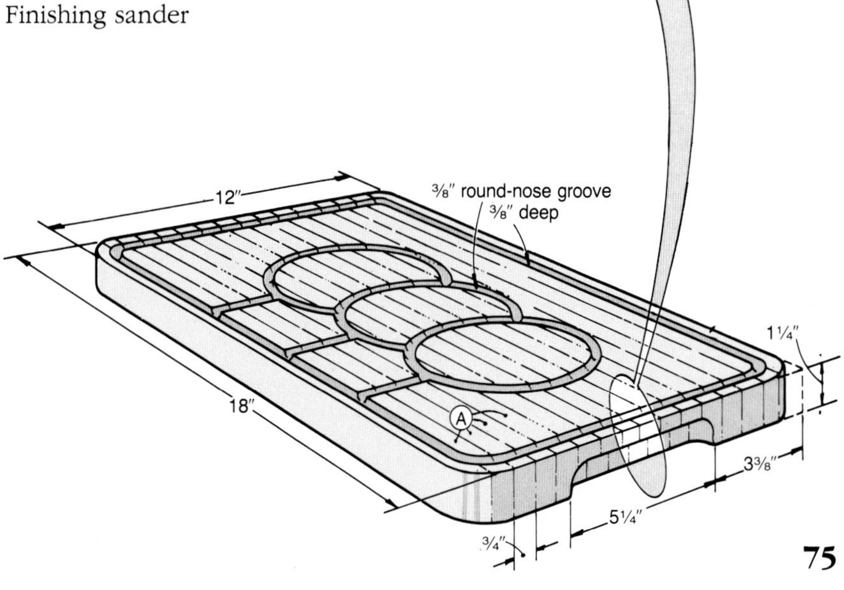
12″
⅜″ round-nose groove
⅜″ deep
1¼″
18″
A
3⅜″
5¼″
¾″

Note: *We built the project using the tools listed. You may be able to substitute other tools or equipment for listed items you don't have. Additional common hand tools and clamps may be required to complete the project.*

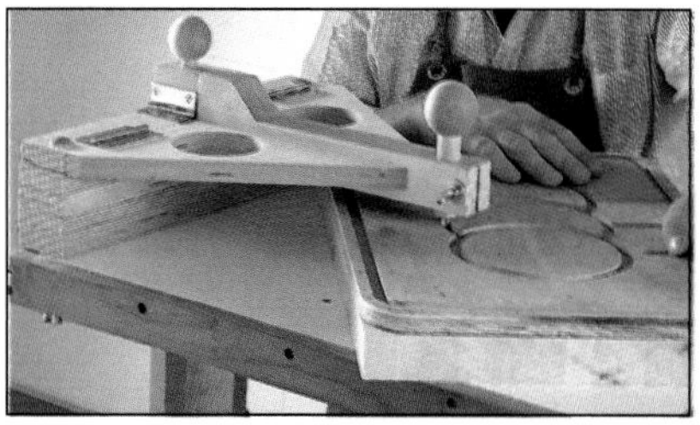

DELTA-WING PIN-ROUTING ATTACHMENT

Note: *The attachment shown* above *was originally built to fit our benchtop router table. If your router table is smaller, you'll need to shorten the arm and reposition the mounting holes. To get the attachment to fit our Heavy-Duty Router Table shown on* page 5, *drill the*

continued

STYLIZED MEAT CARVING BOARD
continued

mounting holes in the pin-routing attachment that will align with the mounting holes in the worktop.

Start with the arm and wings

1. To make the arm (A), cut two pieces of ¾" birch to 2¾×16" (we used Baltic birch plywood). Glue and clamp the pieces together face-to-face.

2. Scrape off the excess glue, and then trim or plane the edges for a 2⅝" finished width. Trim the arm to length (11¼"). Save the scrap—you'll use it later for the hold-down (D).

3. Bore a ¾" hole 1⅛" from one end, centered from side to side, in the arm where shown on the Exploded View drawing *below*. Drill a ¼" hole perpendicular to the ¾" hole ⅜" from the same end.

4. Using a bandsaw, cut the arm to the shape shown on the drawing, and sand smooth. Cut a ⅛" kerf 2¼" long centered on the joint line between the two A's, again referring to the drawing.

5. To make the wings (B), cut a piece of plywood to 7×9⁷⁄₁₆" long. Draw a diagonal across it, and cut down the center of the line to form the two wings. Cut a 3"-diameter

hole in each wing where located on the drawing.

6. Cut or rout a ¾" stopped groove ⅜" deep and 8⅞" long, centered along both side edges of the arm. (We clamped a stop to the rip fence and made our grooves on the tablesaw with a dado blade. If you follow this process, sand the front edge of each wing to match the radiused end of the stopped groove.

7. Glue and clamp the wings into the grooves in the arm (for clamping, we used a handscrew clamp and positioned the clamping parts in the 3" wing holes). Make sure the back edges of the wings and arm are straight and flush. Also check that the wings are level with each other.

Make the support assembly

1. Cut four spacers and the top support (C) to size. Dry-clamp the five pieces together with the edges and ends flush. Then drill a ⅜" hole

through each end of the lamination where dimensioned on the drawing. Remove the top support, reclamp the four spacers, and enlarge the holes in the spacers with a ½" drill bit.

Bill of Materials					
Part	**Finished Size***			**Mat.**	**Qty.**
	T	**W**	**L**		
A* arm	1½"	2⅝"	11¼"	LB	1
B* wing	¾"	6⅝"	8⅞"	B	2
C support/ spacer	¾"	2"	14"	B	5
D* hold-down	1½"	1½"	2"	LB	1

*Parts marked with an * are cut larger initially, then trimmed to finished size. Please read the instructions before cutting.

Material Key: LB–laminated birch, B–birch
Supplies: 2–⅜×6" carriage bolts with flat washer and wing nuts, ¼×2" carriage bolt with flat washer and wing nut, ¼×2½" carriage bolt for alignment pin, ⅜×2" carriage bolt for guide pin, 2–1¾×2½" fast-pin hinges with mounting screws, 2×2" fast-pin hinge with mounting screws, 1½" wooden ball, 2–1¾" wooden balls, ½" dowel, ¾" dowel, epoxy, finish.

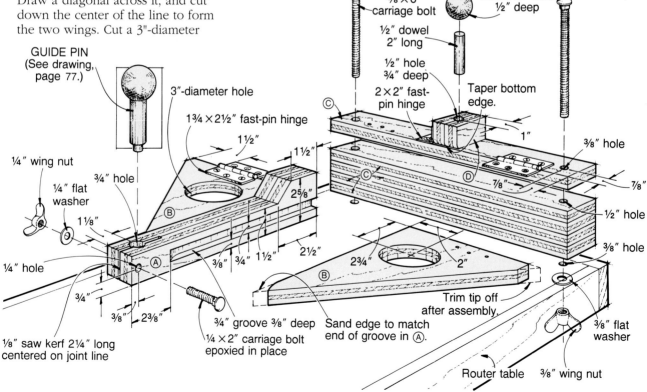

GUIDE PIN (See drawing, page 77.)

⅜ × 6" carriage bolt

1½" wooden ball with a ½" hole ½" deep

½" dowel 2" long

½" hole ¾" deep

2 × 2" fast-pin hinge

Taper bottom edge.

3"-diameter hole

1¾ × 2½" fast-pin hinge

1½"

1½"

1"

⅜" hole

⅞"

¼" wing nut

¼" flat washer

1⅛"

2⅝"

7⅞"

½" hole

⅜" hole

¼" hole

¾"

¾" hole

⅜" ⅜"

¾" 1½"

2½"

2¾"

2"

3/8" 2⅜"

⅛" saw kerf 2¼" long centered on joint line

¾" groove ⅜" deep

¼ × 2" carriage bolt epoxied in place

Sand edge to match end of groove in Ⓐ.

Trim tip off after assembly.

⅜" flat washer

Router table

⅜" wing nut

2. Cut the hold-down (D) to size from the scrap left over from the arm lamination. Bore a ½" hole ¾" deep in the hold-down where shown on the Exploded View drawing. Sand a slight taper on the bottom front edge of the hold-down. The taper makes it easier for the hold-down to force the arm down when routing.

3. Clamp a 1½" wooden ball (available from toy-part suppliers) in a handscrew clamp. Bore a ½" hole ½" deep into it. Cut a piece of ½" dowel to 2". Glue one end of the dowel into the hole in the ball, and the other end into the hold-down.

Construct the guide and alignment pins

Note: The alignment pin aligns the attachment with the router collet. You can use the alignment pin as a guide when routing with ¼"-diameter bits. The guide pin, when positioned in the arm, tracks the template pattern when routing.

1. To make the alignment pin, illustrated *below left*, cut a piece of ¾" dowel to 4⅞" long. Using a drill guide block (see Drill Guide Block drawing, *below right*, for details on how to make one), drill a ¼" hole 1½" deep, centered in the end of the ¾" dowel. (We fit one end of the alignment pin in the ¾" hole in the guide block. Then we used the

¼" hole in the guide block to center the drill bit into the end of the alignment pin.)

2. Cut the head off a ¼x2½" carriage bolt. Epoxy the threaded bolt into the hole in the dowel so 1" of the bolt protrudes. File a round-over on the protruding end of the bolt.

3. Clamp a 1¾" wooden ball in a handscrew, and bore a ¾" hole ⅞" deep into the ball. Glue the ball onto the end of the dowel.

4. To make the guide pin, repeat steps 1–3 above, using a ⅜x2" carriage bolt, a drill guide block with a ⅜" hole, and the Guide Pin drawing, *below*.

Assemble, finish, and mount the attachment

1. Center the arm and wing assembly against the front edge of the top support. Clamp them together, drill hinge holes, and hinge the assembly to the top support. (To ensure a snug fit between the wing assembly and top support, drill the hinge holes in the top support slightly off-center toward the back.) Trim the wing ends flush with the ends of the top support.

2. Position the hold-down on the top support, align it with the arm, and clamp into place. Drill mounting holes, and hinge the hold-down to the top support firmly against the back edge of the arm.

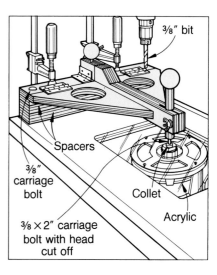

Spacers

⅜" carriage bolt

Collet

Acrylic

⅜ × 2" carriage bolt with head cut off

⅜" bit

3. Place the alignment pin into the ¾" hole in the arm. Epoxy a ¼x2" carriage bolt in the ¼" hole at the kerfed end of the arm, and attach a flat washer and wing nut to the bolt to hold it secure until the epoxy dries. Finish the pin router as desired. (We disassembled the parts, masked off the hinges, and applied polyurethane to the supports, wing assembly and pins.)

4. Raise your table-mounted router so the collet protrudes slightly above the surface of the table. Position the pin-routing attachment (with a couple of spaces beneath it) so the alignment pin fits into the collet as shown in the illustration *above*. Clamp the pin router to the router table. Using the holes in the spacers as guides, drill two ⅜" holes through the router table. Fasten the routing attachment to the router table with a pair of carriage bolts.

Project Tool List
Tablesaw
    Dado blade or dado set
Bandsaw
Portable drill
Drill press
    Bits: ¼", ⅜", ½", ¾"
    Holesaw or circle cutter

Note: We built the project using the tools listed. You may be able to substitute other tools or equipment for listed items you don't have. Additional common hand tools and clamps may be required to complete the project.

ALIGNMENT PIN   **GUIDE PIN**
SECTION VIEW

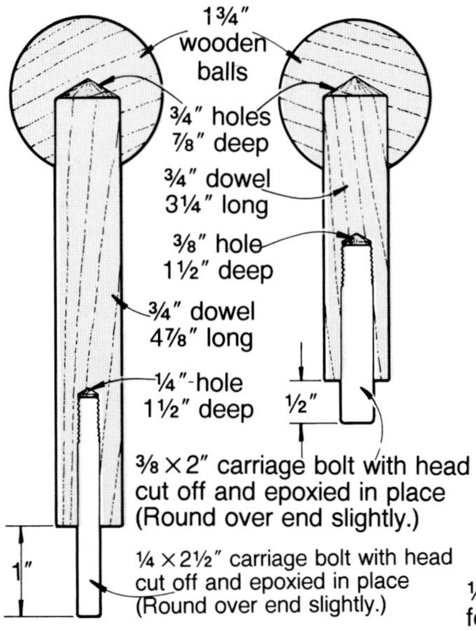

1¾" wooden balls

¾" holes ⅞" deep

¾" dowel 3¼" long

⅜" hole 1½" deep

¾" dowel 4⅞" long

¼"-hole 1½" deep

½"

⅜ × 2" carriage bolt with head cut off and epoxied in place (Round over end slightly.)

¼ × 2½" carriage bolt with head cut off and epoxied in place (Round over end slightly.)

1"

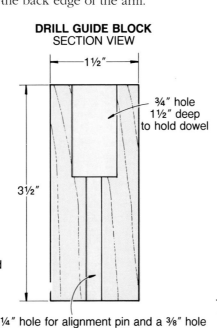

DRILL GUIDE BLOCK
SECTION VIEW

1½"

¾" hole 1½" deep to hold dowel

3½"

¼" hole for alignment pin and a ⅜" hole for guide pin to guide drill bit

LAZY SUSAN

Invite guests over and you can pretty much predict where they'll end up—within arm's reach of the munchies. That's when you need our full-service lazy Susan. Six deep compartments routed in mahogany hold crackers, nuts, and other popular snacks, while the eight-inch maple cutting board works great for slicing cheese or sausage. For guaranteed success, let our templates guide your router.

First, make the laminations and the templates

1. To make the tray (A) as shown in the Exploded View drawing *opposite*, rip and crosscut 22–¾" mahogany pieces to 1⅚×16". Apply glue to the wide face of each piece (except the outside faces of the two outerpieces) and clamp them together, making a 16×16½" rectangle. Remove the clamps after the glue dries, and belt-sand both the top and bottom surfaces to a 1¼" thickness.

2. For the cutting board (B), cut 11–1¹⁄₁₆×8¼" strips from ¾"-thick maple. Apply glue to the wide faces of each piece as before, assemble, and clamp the lamination. After the glue dries, remove the clamps and belt-sand the maple to a 1" thickness. Set the lamination aside for now.

3. Make a photocopy of the Full-Sized Template pattern on *page 81*. Cut out the template. (We left a ¼" margin around the outline so the black line remained.)

4. Next, cut six 9" squares out of ¼"-thick plywood. (We started with a 24×48" piece.) Using double-faced tape, stack the pieces together. Spray the back of the template pattern with adhesive, and stick it to the top square on the stack. Cut the wedge-shaped pieces to shape with your scrollsaw. (We cut slightly wide of the line, and sanded to the pattern line with a disk sander.) Now, drill the three ¹⁄₁₆" pilot holes in the wedge-shaped pieces where marked on the pattern. Switch to a ½" bit and drill

a start hole through the area to be cut out.

5. Thread a scrollsaw blade through the ½" hole, and attach it to your scrollsaw. Cut out the inside of the template as shown *below*.

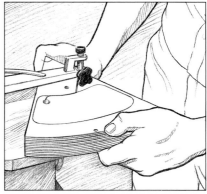

6. Attach a 2"-diameter drum sander to your drill press, and gang-sand the walls of the cutout area to the line. Separate the templates and remove the tape. Countersink the screw holes in each template.

7. Cut a piece of ¼" plywood to 12" square. Mark the centerpoint. Drive a finish nail into the center and cut it off so ½" protrudes.

8. To aid you in cutting the 8¼"-diameter circle in the square (and to rout the other circular cuts), make the router trammel shown on *page 81*, and mount it on your router. Next, chuck a ¼" straight bit in your router's collet, and set it to cut ¼" deep. Place the square on a larger piece of scrap plywood, and place pivot hole W on the trammel base over the pivot nail. Now, turn on the router, lower the bit into the plywood, and rotate the router couterclockwise around the pivot to make the cut. Drill and countersink a ¹⁄₁₆" pilot hole ½" in from each corner of the plywood square. Save the square and the disk you cut out.

9. Square the ends of the mahogany lamination, and then draw diagonal lines to locate the centerpoint. Mark the point with an awl. Next, arrange the six wedge-shaped templates in a circle around the centerpoint. Now, drive the screws through the pilot holes in the templates to fasten them to the lamination. (We used #3x½" flathead wood screws.)

Next, rout the tray compartments

Note: *To rout the compartments in the tray, you'll need a special bit called a 3 from 1, and a ⅝" guide bushing for your router. See the Buying Guide for a mail-order source for both items.*

1. Remove the trammel base from your router. Replace the original base and mount a ⅝" guide bushing to it. Chuck the 3-from-1 bit in the collet and adjust the router so the bit cuts ¼" deep. Rout all six compartments to this depth as shown *below*. (When cutting, guide the router with steady, even pressure against the walls.) Stop the router, readjust the depth to ½", then rout all compartments again. Finally, set the bit to cut ¾" deep and repeat the process.

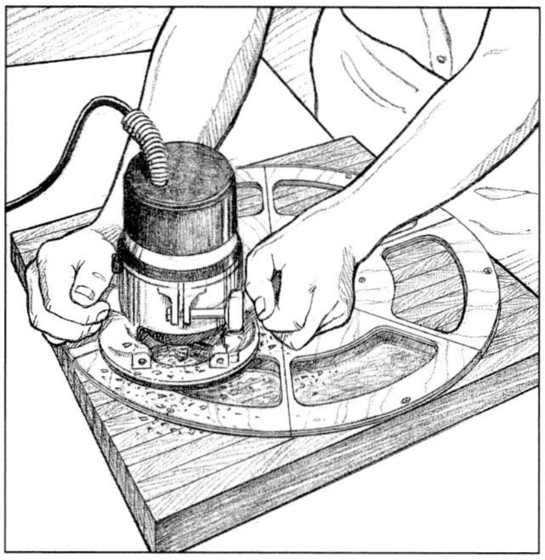

Carefully smooth the bottom of each compartment with the router. When finished, remove the templates.

2. Using a compass and the center point on the mahogany lamination, draw an 8¼"-diameter circle. Next drill a ¹⁄₁₆" hole through the lamination's centerpoint. You'll use this same hole as the pivot point for the bearing recess on the *underside* of the lamination.

3. Place the plywood square you cut earlier over the lamination, aligning the hole with the 8¼"-diameter circle you just drew. Now, screw the square to the lamination.

continued

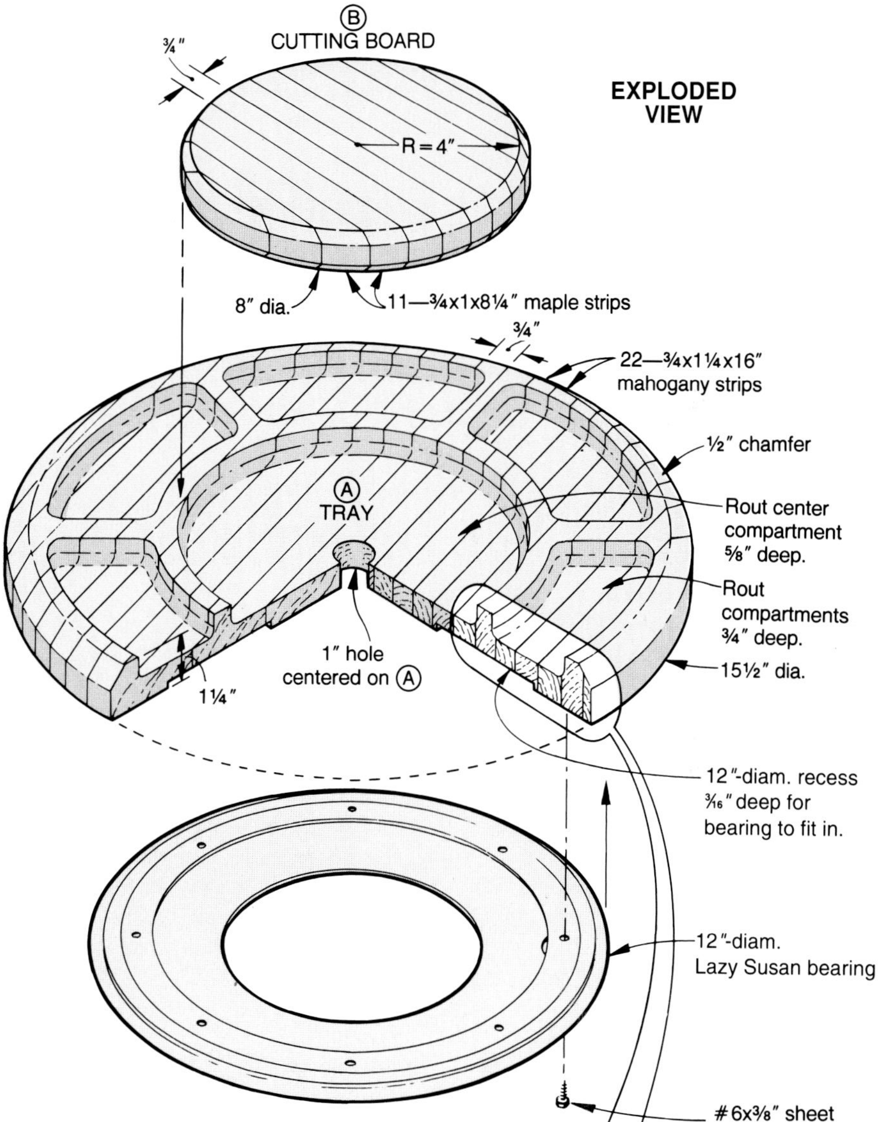

Ⓑ CUTTING BOARD
EXPLODED VIEW
¾"
R=4"
8" dia.
11—¾x1x8¼" maple strips
¾"
22—¾x1¼x16" mahogany strips
½" chamfer
Ⓐ TRAY
Rout center compartment ⅝" deep.
Rout compartments ¾" deep.
1" hole centered on Ⓐ
1¼"
15½" dia.
12"-diam. recess ³⁄₁₆" deep for bearing to fit in.
12"-diam. Lazy Susan bearing
#6x⅜" sheet metal screw (one shown, four required)

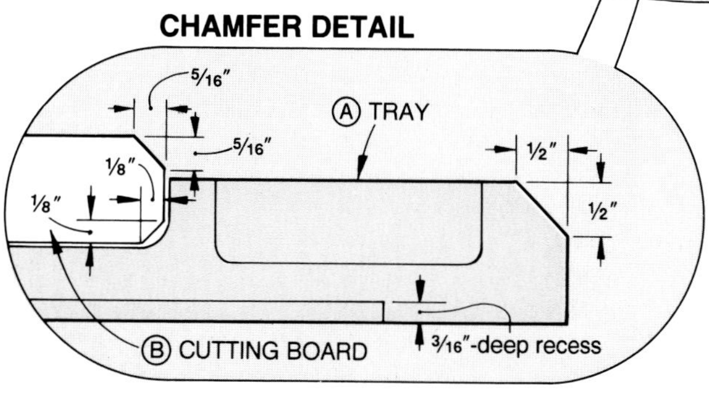

CHAMFER DETAIL
⁵⁄₁₆"
⁵⁄₁₆"
⅛"
⅛"
Ⓐ TRAY
½"
½"
Ⓑ CUTTING BOARD
³⁄₁₆"-deep recess

Bill of Materials

Part	Finished Size* T	W	L	Mat.	Qty.
A*	1¼"		15½" dia.	MH	1
B*	1"		8" dia.	M	1

Parts marked with an * are cut to finished size from laminations. Please read the instructions before cutting.

Material Key: MH—mahogany, M—maple
Supplies: 4—self-adhesive bumpers, 16—#3 x ½" flathead wood screws, 4—#6 x ⅜" sheet metal screws, photocopy of template pattern, ¼" plywood, finish.

LAZY SUSAN
continued

4. Using your router and the 3 from 1 bit, make a ⁵⁄₁₆"-deep cut around the circumference of the template. Then, set the bit to cut ⅝" deep. Make the deeper pass around the circumference to form a neat outside cut, and to set the finish depth for the center compartment.

5. To help steady your router while routing out the center compartment, take the ¼"-thick plywood disk you saved earlier, and cut away 2" of it. Next, place it back in the opening as shown in drawing A *below*. Attach it temporarily with small brads. Now, leaving your router at the ⅝" depth, slowly and carefully rout out the wood in the exposed area within the routed ring. When you've done that, slice off another 2" from the ¼" disk, and rout the exposed mahogany within the ring. Carefully finish the bottom before moving on to the next cut because you can't go back later to clean it up. Repeat the process until you end up at the point shown in drawing B, *below right*. Then, remove the last of the plywood disk and finish routing the mahogany remaining in the ring. Finally, remove the template from the lamination.

Now, prepare the bottom

1. Place the routed lamination upside down on a piece of scrap plywood. Drive a finish nail in the drilled center hole for the pivot and

shorten it to ½". To make the 15½"-diameter cut, use your router, a ¼" straight bit, and the trammel base. Place hole X on the trammel base over the pivot nail. Make several cutting passes, lowering the bit ¼" after each round, until you cut through the lamination.

2. Next, rout the ³⁄₁₆"-deep recess in the *bottom* side for the lazy-Susan bearing. (We used our router, a ¼" straight bit, and pivot holes Y1 through Y12 on the trammel base.)

3. Using a Forstner or spade bit, bore the 1" hole in the center of the tray. (Back the tray with scrap to prevent chip-out.)

Shape the cutting board and chamfer the edges

1. Take the maple lamination you made earlier, and square the ends. Turn it upside down, and mark the centerpoint. Drive a finish nail into the center to serve as a pivot for the trammel. Cut off the nail so only ½" protrudes. Next, place the maple on a piece of scrap plywood. Now, using your router, a ¼" straight bit, and pivot hole Y5 on the trammel base, cut the lamination to shape.

2. Mount your router to a router table, and chuck a ½" chamfer bit in the collet. Raise the bit just enough to cut a ⅛" chamfer along the *bottom* edge of the round maple board. (See the Chamfer detail on

the Exploded View drawing on *page 79*.) Make the cut. Then, raise the bit, turn the board over, and adjust the router to cut a ⁵⁄₁₆" chamfer along the *top* edge of the maple board. Finally, cut a ½" chamfer along the top outside edge of the mahogany tray.

Now, finish the tray

1. Finish-sand the tray and cutting board. Then, apply nontoxic finishes of your choice to the two parts. (We applied three coats of satin polyurethne to the tray, and salad bowl oil to the cutting board.)

2. Screw the lazy-Susan bearing in the recess on the underside. (See the Buying Guide for our source We also applied self-adhesive bumpers [available at many hardware stores] to the bearing to protect table tops from the metal bearing.)

Buying Guide

• **3 from 1 router bit.** ¼" shaft, catalog no. 06V22. For current prices, contact Woodcraft, 41 Atlantic Ave., P.O. Box 4000, Woburn, MA 01888. Phone 800-225-1153

• **Router guide bushing set.** Includes a universal router, base plate; ⁵⁄₁₆"-, ⁷⁄₁₆"-short and long lengths, and ⅝"-diameter bushings. Catalog no. 11V12. For current prices, contact Woodcraft, address *above*.

• **Lazy-Susan bearing.** Round, 12"-diameter, ball bearing. Catalog no. 02251. For current prices, contact Woodcraft, address *above*.

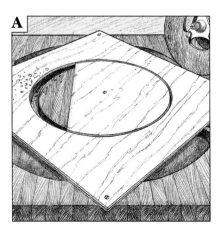

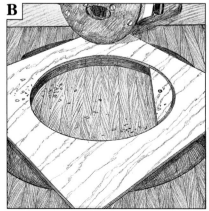

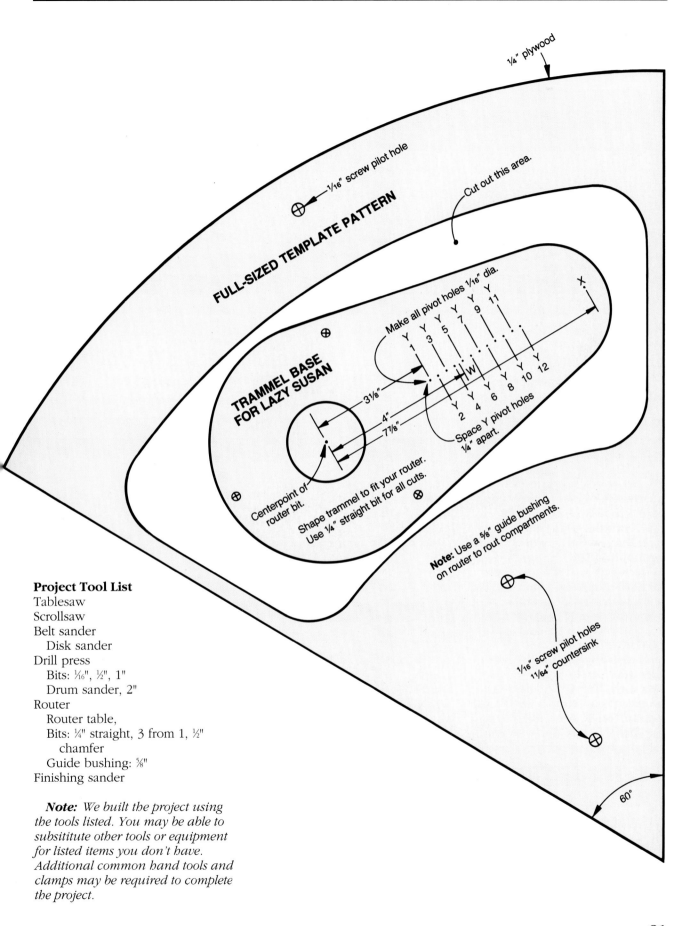

¼" plywood

¹⁄₁₆" screw pilot hole

FULL-SIZED TEMPLATE PATTERN

Cut out this area.

TRAMMEL BASE FOR LAZY SUSAN

Make all pivot holes ¹⁄₁₆" dia.

X

Y 1 Y 3 Y 5 Y 7 Y 9 Y 11

W

Y 2 Y 4 Y 6 Y 8 Y 10 Y 12

Space Y pivot holes ¼" apart.

3⅛"
4"
7⅞"

Centerpoint of router bit.

Shape trammel to fit your router. Use ¼" straight bit for all cuts.

Note: Use a ⅝" guide bushing on router to rout compartments.

¹⁄₁₆" screw pilot holes ¹¹⁄₆₄" countersink

60°

Project Tool List
Tablesaw
Scrollsaw
Belt sander
  Disk sander
Drill press
  Bits: ¹⁄₁₆", ½", 1"
  Drum sander, 2"
Router
  Router table,
  Bits: ¼" straight, 3 from 1, ½"
    chamfer
  Guide bushing: ⅝"
Finishing sander

  Note: *We built the project using the tools listed. You may be able to subsititute other tools or equipment for listed items you don't have. Additional common hand tools and clamps may be required to complete the project.*

MUSICAL TONE BOX

Early wooden drums, found on almost every continent, were typically hollowed-out logs. Our ancestors used them for ceremony and communication. Though the modern version, shown *above,* offers the same rich sounds, it's much better looking, and a lot more fun to make. Expert tone-box designer Gary Damaskos recommends using ¾"-thick native hardwoods for the box sides and top. In this project we'll introduce you to dovetail joinery. If you'd rather avoid the dovetail joints, Gary assured us that butt and half-lap joints on the box work equally well.

We'll start by cutting the box parts

1. Select the wood for the tone box, picking the straightest, flattest boards you can. (We chose cherry for the top, maple for the sides and ends, and birch plywood for the bottom.) See the Cutting diagram and Bill of Materials *opposite.*

2. Square the maple stock, and then rip it to 4½" wide. Crosscut two 15¼"-long pieces from the board for the sides (A), and two 6½"-long pieces for the ends (B). Crosscut two 6"-long pieces to use for testing the dovetail setup later.

3. For the top (C), square the ¾" cherry stock, and then rip and crosscut one 6½x16" piece from it.

4. Cut the ¼" plywood bottom (D) to 6½x16". (We purchased a 12x24" piece at a hobby shop.)

Next, cut the dovetails

1. Assemble your dovetail jig. (For this box, we used a Vermont-American jig with its ½" flush-joint template, and a ½" dovetail bit.) If you are not very familiar with dovetailing, we recommend you read the manual that comes with your jig before attempting to rout the joints. Follow the manual and set up your jig to cut ½" dovetail joints.

2. To orient the tone box for dovetailing, think of the box sides (A) as drawer sides, and the box ends (B) as drawer fronts. Label the pieces, mark the inside faces, and number the mating corners as shown on the Exploded View drawing *opposite.*

3. Use the two 6"-long maple pieces you cut earlier and make a test joint of corner 1. First, clamp the left or *front side* test piece *vertically* in the jig, with the *inside* surface facing *out.* Butt it against the left side stop (as you face it). Extend the piece ½" above the top of the base. Next, place the *end* piece *horizontally* under the template, with the *inside* surface facing up. Butt it against the side piece and the left top stop, and clamp. Now, move the side piece up flush with the top surface of the end piece as shown *below,* and clamp.

4. Install a ⁷⁄₁₆" guide bushing and a ½" dovetail bit on your router. Set the bit to the depth specified in the manual. Rout the joint, cutting from left to right.

5. Remove both pieces from the jig, and assemble the joint to test the fit. If the joint fits too loosely, increase the bit's depth slightly (about ¹⁄₆₄"). If it fits too tightly, decrease the bit depth. If the pins (triangular-shaped fingers left on the ends after routing) recess into the sockets (triangular-shaped openings cut into ends), adjust the template forward (toward you) on the base. If the pins protrude from the sockets, move the template farther back on the base so the bit

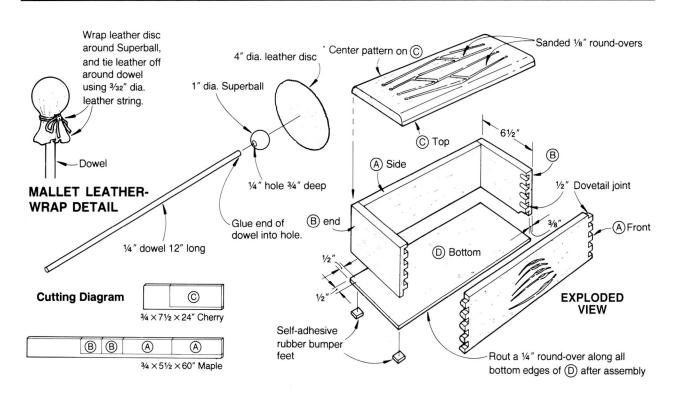

Wrap leather disc around Superball, and tie leather off around dowel using ³⁄₃₂" dia. leather string.

— Dowel

MALLET LEATHER-WRAP DETAIL

¼" dowel 12" long

1" dia. Superball

4" dia. leather disc

¼" hole ¾" deep

Glue end of dowel into hole.

Cutting Diagram

Ⓒ
¾ × 7½ × 24" Cherry

Ⓑ Ⓑ Ⓐ Ⓐ
¾ × 5½ × 60" Maple

Center pattern on Ⓒ

Sanded ⅛" round-overs

Ⓒ Top

Ⓐ Side

6½"

Ⓑ

½" Dovetail joint

⅜"

Ⓐ Front

Ⓑ end

Ⓓ Bottom

½"

½"

Self-adhesive rubber bumper feet

EXPLODED VIEW

Rout a ¼" round-over along all bottom edges of Ⓓ after assembly

Bill of Materials				
Part	Finished Size		Mat.	Qty.
	T	W	L		
A sides	¾"	4½"	15¼"	M	2
B ends	¾"	4½"	6½"	M	2
C top	¾"	6½"	16"	C	1
D bottom	¼"	6½"	16"	BP	1

Material Key: M—maple, C—cherry, BP—birch plywood.
Supplies: 2—1"-diameter Superballs, ¼" dowel, kidskin leather, ³⁄₃₂" leather string, 4—self-adhesive rubber feet.

can cut farther into the end piece. Make the adjustments, and retest the joints until correct.

6. Dovetail the parts. Rout corner 1, and then corner 3 on the left side of the jig. Next, switch to the right side of the jig and make a test joint to check it. Rout corner 2, and then corner 4 on the right side.

Cut the slots next

1. Using carbon paper or a photo-copier, make copies of the speaker and top patterns on *pages 84–85*.

2. Lightly mark centerlines for both length and width on the front side piece. Apply spray adhesive to the back of the speaker pattern. Adhere the pattern to the front piece, aligning the pattern center-lines with those on the front. (You may trace the pattern directly onto the piece.)

3. Using the same technique, transfer the top pattern to the top surface of the cherry piece.

4. With a ⅛" bit in your drill press, carefully drill through the five start holes marked on the speaker pattern. (We drilled several overlapping holes to accommodate the saw's blade. We also backed the piece with scrap when drilling to prevent chip-out.) Next, clamp the board, and using a portable jigsaw, saw the five lines as shown at *right*. Always let the saw's blade come to a stop before lifting it from the slot. Make these slots one blade wide except where pattern shows them wider.

5. Saw the slots in the top piece. (We used a ⁵⁄₁₆" bit to drill the eight end holes. Then, we made the long, straight cuts between the end holes, and finished by making the diagonal connecting cuts.)

6. Sand the edges of the slots in both pieces as shown at *right* to round them over. (Shaping the edges of these cuts requires a lot of sanding. We used ¾"-wide strips cut from a sanding belt. You can use strips of cloth- or paper-backed

sandpaper, and then apply strips of masking tape to the sandpaper to make them more durable.) Start with 100- or 120-grit sandpaper and finish with 220-grit sandpaper.

continued

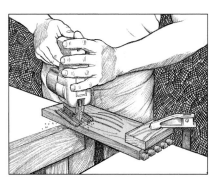

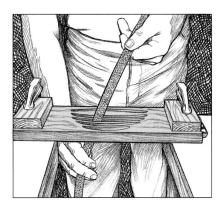

MUSICAL TONE BOX
continued

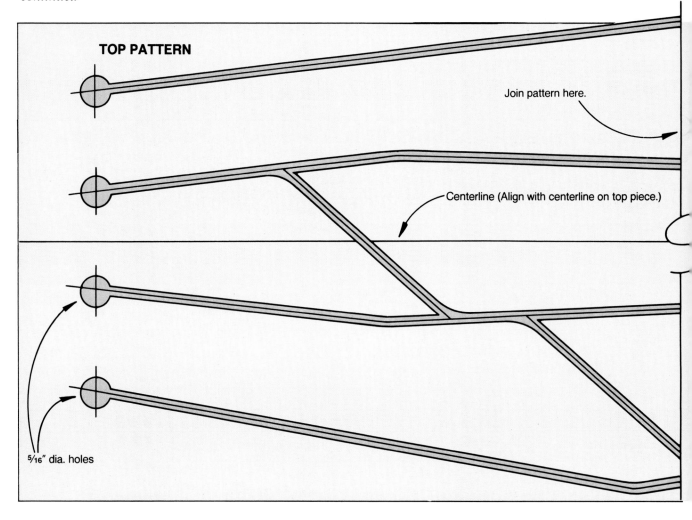

TOP PATTERN

Join pattern here.

Centerline (Align with centerline on top piece.)

5/16" dia. holes

One box, now ready for assembly

1. Apply glue (we used yellow woodworker's glue) to the dovetail joints, and assemble the sides and ends. Tap the joints tight with a mallet and block. Wipe off any glue squeeze-out with a damp cloth. Clamp until the glue cures. (We placed small wood pads between the clamps and the wood parts to prevent marring the wood.)

2. Glue the top and bottom pieces to the side assembly, and clamp. Wipe off glue squeeze-out. Remove the clamps after the glue dries. Now, belt-sand all edges flush.

3. With a router and a ½" round-over bit, rout the edges along the top. Switch to a ¼" round bit and round over the edges along the bottom. Do not round over the edges of the sides or ends.

4. Make two mallets, using the Mallet drawing on *page 83*. (We bought the balls at a toy store.)

With scissors, cut two 4"-diameter leather discs. (We used kidskin purchased at a crafts supply store.) Wrap the leather around the balls as shown on the Leather Wrap detail on *page 83*, and tie the knots.

Finish the tone box

1. Finish-sand all surfaces. (We used 150- and 220-grit sandpaper.) Hand-sand to round the corners.

2. Apply the finish. (We used Deft brand Danish Oil. The designer recommends not using stiff finishes such as lacquer.) Pour a cup of the oil inside the box, and turn it on its ends and sides to wet the inside surfaces. Drain out the excess oil. Wipe finish on the outside, keeping the surfaces wet for 30 minutes. Wipe off the excess oil and let the wood dry.

3. Apply self-adhesive feet to the bottom. (We purchased a set of four at a local hardware store.)

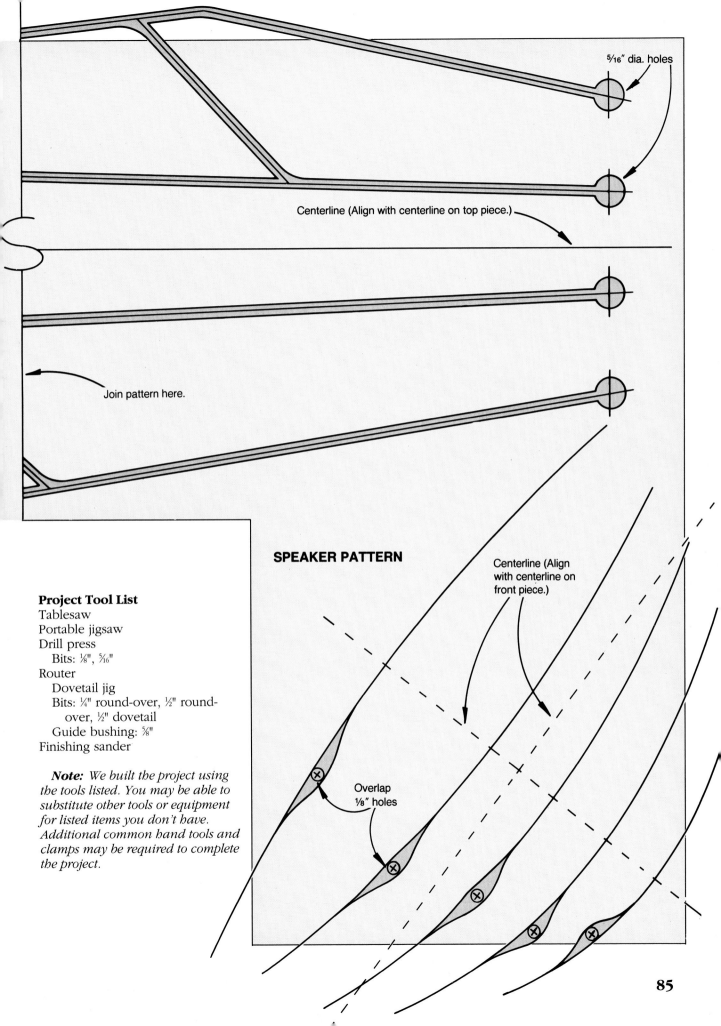

5/16" dia. holes

Centerline (Align with centerline on top piece.)

Join pattern here.

SPEAKER PATTERN

Centerline (Align with centerline on front piece.)

Overlap 1/8" holes

Project Tool List
Tablesaw
Portable jigsaw
Drill press
   Bits: 1/8", 5/16"
Router
   Dovetail jig
   Bits: 1/4" round-over, 1/2" round-over, 1/2" dovetail
   Guide bushing: 5/8"
Finishing sander

Note: *We built the project using the tools listed. You may be able to substitute other tools or equipment for listed items you don't have. Additional common hand tools and clamps may be required to complete the project.*

TAMBOURIFFIC ROLLTOP RECIPE BOX

Whether you're building a rolltop desk or a simple box for storing recipe cards, the process for making tambour remains the same. After you've made this one, we encourage you to try more challenging tambour projects in the future.

Let's make the box sides first

1. Trace or photocopy the Template pattern on *page 89.* Cut out the pattern with scissors.

2. Make the side template by first squaring a scrap piece of ¾"-thick stock measuring at least 5x6". Adhere the paper pattern to the scrap, aligning the square corner and adjacent sides of the pattern and the scrap. (We applied spray adhesive to the back of the paper pattern.) Saw and sand the template to shape. From the same piece of scrap, cut a ⅝x3" piece to serve as an extension of the template. Temporarily screw the extension to the template.

Note: *This project requires ½"- and ⅜"-thick stock. Plane or resaw thicker stock to this thickness.*

3. Rip and crosscut a ½x5x14" piece of oak, and clamp it to your work surface. (When routing the left box side, we placed the clamp toward the opposite end of the piece so it wouldn't interfere, and

then moved it to the other end when we routed the right box side.) Rip a 10" length of scrap wood to ⅝" wide and crosscut it into two 5" lengths. With hot-melt glue, tack the ⅝"-wide spacer strips at and parallel to each end of the board.

4. Apply double-faced tape to the underside of your template and position it on the board, butting the marked front edge of the template against the spacer along the left side, and aligning the bottom of the extension with the bottom edge of the board as shown *opposite, lower left.* Now, remove the left-side spacer.

5. Attach a ½" O.D. guide bushing to your router's base. Chuck a ¼" straight bit in the collet, and set it to cut ¼" below the template. (We tested all router settings on scrap first.) If you use a different-sized bushing, you'll need to adjust the dimensions of the template.

6. To rout the tambour groove (Cut 1) on the inside face of the *left* side piece (see the Side drawing and the Exploded View drawing *opposite* for more details), place the router base on the template, and the bushing against the edge of the template. Next, starting at the lower left corner, rout in about an inch to get beyond the extension, and then stop the router. Remove the extension. Now, rout counterclockwise around the template's perimeter.

7. To rout the *right* side piece, reattach the extension to the template, and then turn the template over and apply double-faced tape to its underside. Set the template, butting the front edge against the spacer and aligning the bottom of the extension with bottom edge of the piece. Position the router, and starting at the lower right corner, rout in about 1" and stop. Now, remove the extension from the template, and continue

routing counterclockwise around the template's perimeter.

8. Remove the template and release the workpiece. Measuring in from the outside edges of the board, crosscut both sides to 6" long. *Do not round the corners yet.*

9. Mount your router in a router table and set the fence, stopblocks, and bit as shown for Cut 2 on the Router Setup drawing on *page 88.* Rout the ¼" slot (Cut 2) along the bottom of the inside face of the left side piece. See the Side drawing for additional information. (To make smooth cuts, we held the piece against the fence and startblock, turned on the router, slowly lowered the piece squarely onto the bit, and then moved the piece to the stopblock to cut the slot.)

10. Reset the fence and stopblocks, as shown in the Cut 3 setup, and rout the slot (Cut 3) along the back of the left side piece.

11. To rout the right side piece, set up the router table as shown on the Router Setup drawing except you reverse the start- and stopblock settings (actually a mirror image of the drawing). Rout slot 2 into the right side piece. Next, reverse the Cut 3 setup, and then rout Slot 3 into the right side piece.

12. Using a compass, scribe the 1¼" radii on the three corners of *continued*

Bill of Materials					
Part	Finished Size			Mat.	Qty.
	T	W	L		
A sides	½"	5"	6"	O	2
B bottom	⅜"	4⅜"	5¾"	O	1
C back	⅜"	2¾"	5¾"	O	1
D front	⅜"	2"	5¾"	O	1
E bar	⅜"	⅝"	4½"	O	1
F pull	⅜"	⅝"	5⅛"	O	1
G slats	3⁄16"	⅜"	5⅝"	O	24

Material Key: O—oak
Supplies: ¼" dowel, canvas, finish.

EXPLODED VIEW

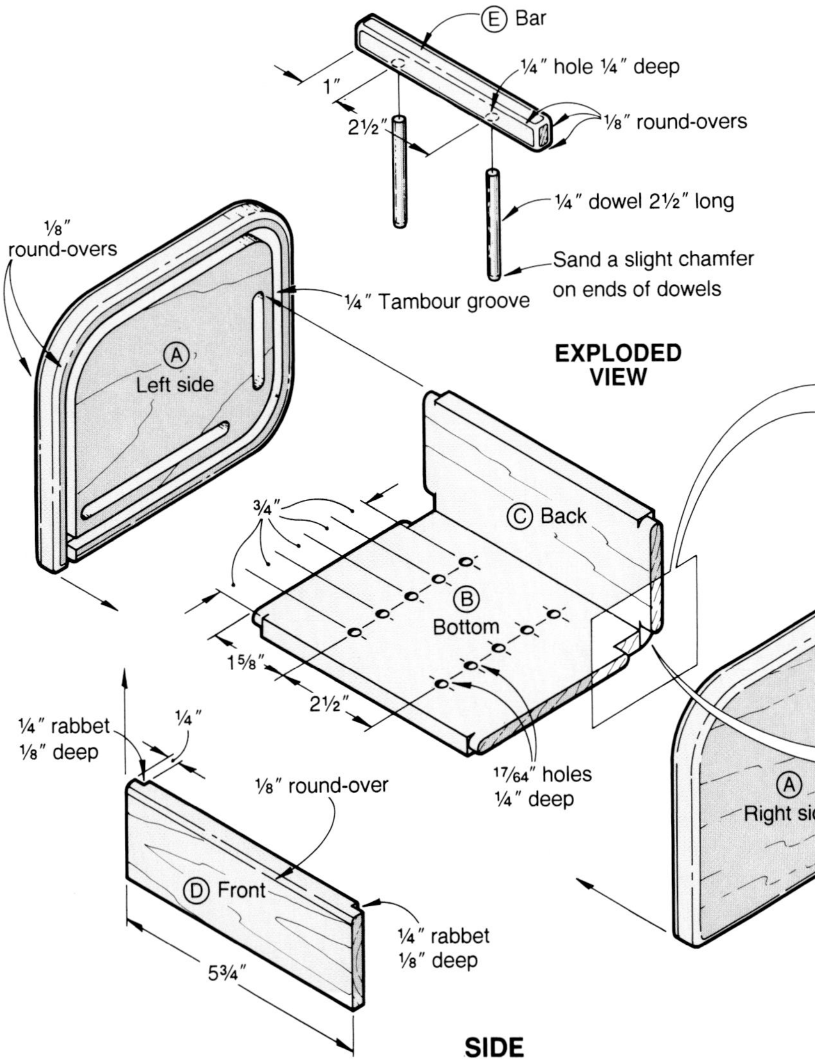

Ⓔ Bar
1″
2½″
¼″ hole ¼″ deep
⅛″ round-overs
¼″ dowel 2½″ long
Sand a slight chamfer on ends of dowels
⅛″ round-overs
¼″ Tambour groove
Ⓐ Left side
EXPLODED VIEW
Ⓒ Back
¾″
Ⓑ Bottom
1⅝″
2½″
17/64″ holes ¼″ deep
¼″ rabbet ⅛″ deep
¼″
⅛″ round-over
Ⓓ Front
5¾″
¼″ rabbet ⅛″ deep
Ⓐ Right side
Note: Install tambour before gluing Ⓓ in place.

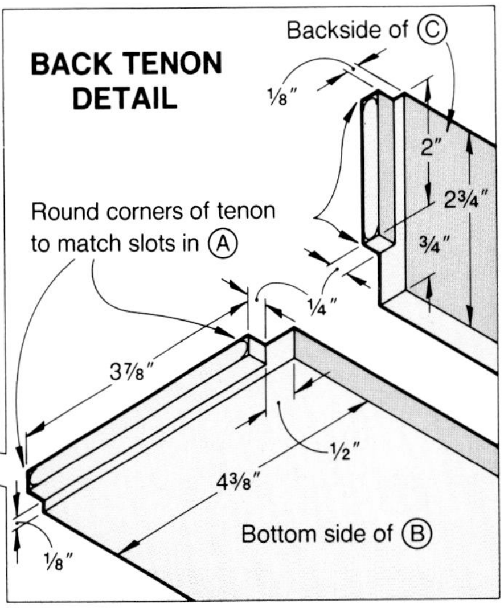

BACK TENON DETAIL
Backside of Ⓒ
⅛″
2″
2¾″
¾″
Round corners of tenon to match slots in Ⓐ
¼″
3⅞″
½″
4⅜″
Bottom side of Ⓑ
⅛″

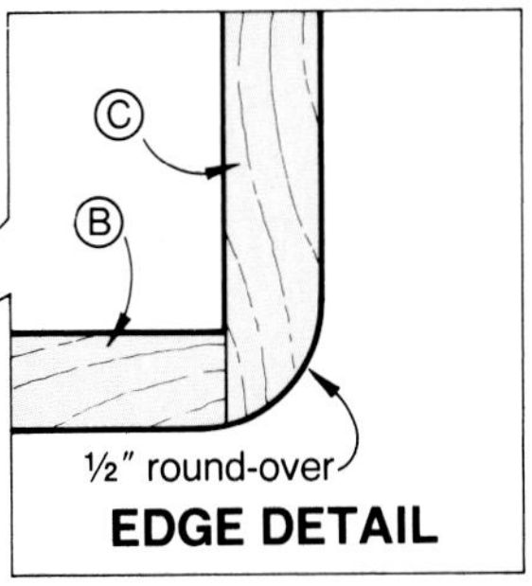

Ⓒ
Ⓑ
½″ round-over
EDGE DETAIL

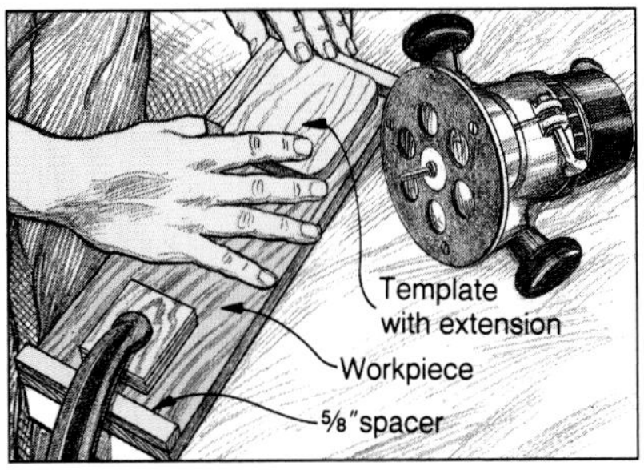

Template with extension
Workpiece
⅝″spacer

CUTTING DIAGRAM

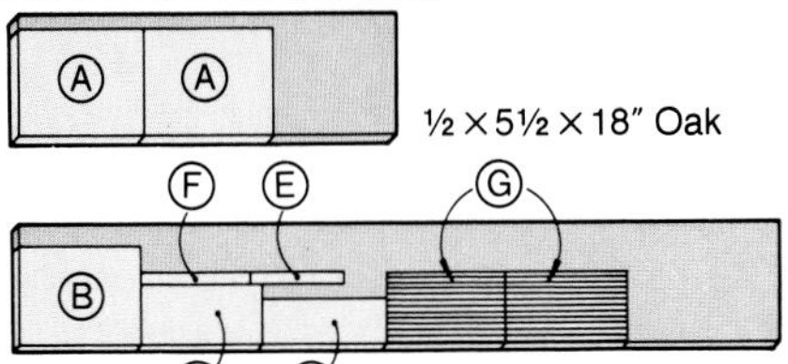

Ⓐ Ⓐ
½ × 5½ × 18″ Oak
Ⓕ Ⓔ Ⓖ
Ⓑ
Ⓒ Ⓓ
⅜ × 5½ × 36″ Oak

SIDE

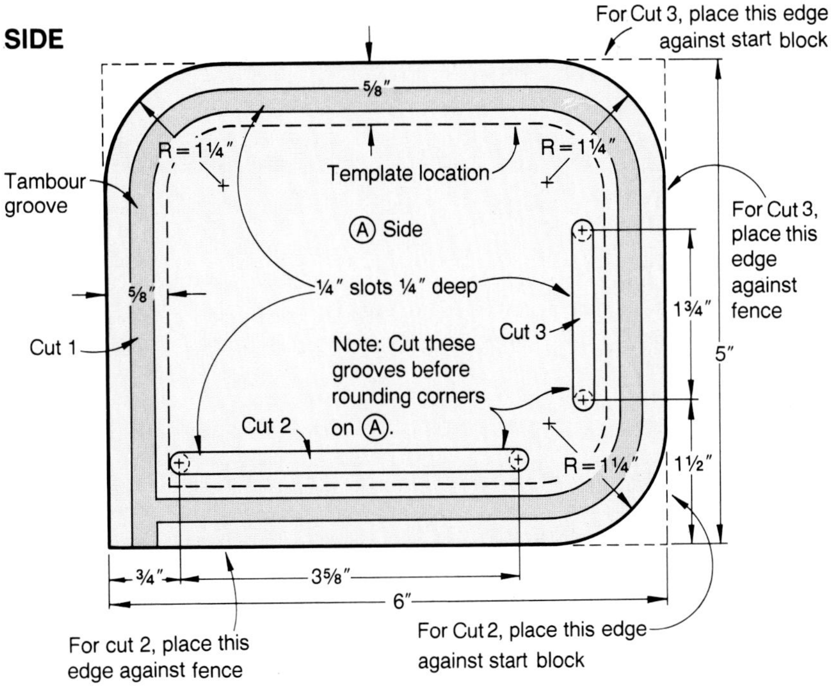

For Cut 3, place this edge against start block
⅝″
R = 1¼″
Template location
R = 1¼″
Tambour groove
Ⓐ Side
For Cut 3, place this edge against fence
⅝″
¼″ slots ¼″ deep
1¾″
5″
Cut 3
Note: Cut these grooves before rounding corners on Ⓐ.
Cut 1
Cut 2
R = 1¼″
1½″
¾″
3⅝″
6″
For cut 2, place this edge against fence
For Cut 2, place this edge against start block

ROLLTOP RECIPE BOX
continued

both side pieces. Bandsaw the corners round, and then sand. (We used our disc sander.)

Next, cut the remaining box parts

1. From ⅜"-thick oak, rip and crosscut the bottom (B) to the size listed in the Bill of Materials. From the remaining piece, rip and cross-cut a ⅝X12" piece and set it aside temporarily. Next, rip and crosscut the back (C), and front (D) to size.

2. Using your table-mounted router and a fence, cut the ¼" rabbets ⅛" deep on the ends of these pieces as shown on the Exploded View drawing, and the Back and Bottom Tenon details on *page 87*. Complete the shaping of the tenons by first rounding them over where shown, and then test-fitting them in the matching slots in the sides. (We filed and sanded the ends of the tenons to fit.)

3. Mark the centerpoints for the holes in the top face of the bottom as dimension on the Exploded View drawing. Now, drill the ¹⁷⁄₆₄" holes. (We drilled them with our drill press.) Finish-sand all parts.

4. Glue and clamp the bottom and back together. (We used yellow woodworker's glue, and held the parts square with small L-shaped corner guides while clamping.) After the glue dries, remove the clamps and corner guides. Now, using a ½" round-over bit, rout the outside joined edge of the two parts as shown in the Edge detail in the Exploded View drawing.

5. Chuck a ⅛" piloted round-over bit in your router. Rout along the inside and outside edges on the two side pieces (A), the 12"-long piece you just cut in Step 1, and the top edges of the front piece (D).

6. Crosscut the bar (E) and tambour pull (F) to length from the 12"-long piece. Drill the two ¼" holes ¼" deep into one edge of the pull as dimensioned on the Exploded View drawing. Sand round-overs on the ends of both parts. Crosscut two 2½" lengths of ¼" dowel. Sand a slight

ROUTER SETUP

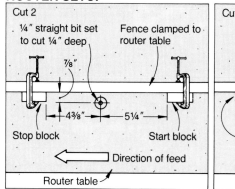

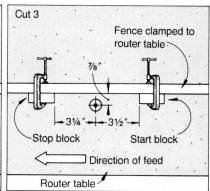

chamfer on the ends of both, then glue the dowels in the holes drilled in the bar.

Make the tambour now

Note: If the slot in your saw's insert causes a problem when you rip the ³⁄₁₆"-thick tambour slats in the next step, make an auxiliary top from ⅛"- or ¼"-thick hardboard. Elevate the blade through it.

1. From the remaining ⅜"-wide stock, rip and crosscut a 12" length. Round over all edges. See the Slat detail associated with the Tambour drawing *opposite*. Next, using your tablesaw, miter gauge with an auxiliary fence, and a spacer block, rip a ³⁄₁₆"-thick slat from each edge. Next, alternate between routing the edges and ripping the strips, until you have 14 tambour slats (2 extra in case of damage). Now, crosscut two 5⅝"-long tambour slats (G) from each piece. Finish-sand all tambour parts.

2. Build a tambour gluing guide by cutting two ¾X¾X12" strips and two ¾X¾X5⅝" strips from scrap. Place waxed paper on a piece of plywood, and then nail the 12" strips over the waxed paper and to the plywood so they are parallel and 5⅝" apart. Now, tack one of the short strips at one end of the two parallel strips, squaring it at the corners.

3. To assemble the tambour, cut a 4⅞X9¼" piece of canvas cloth. Place the canvas on the waxed paper, one end against the wood starting strip and centering it (⅜"

margins) between the side guide strips. (We purchased the canvas at a local fabric store.) Pin down or tack the canvas to the plywood to keep it from moving. Spread white or yellow woodworker's glue uniformly over the surface of the canvas. Now, one by one, lay the tambour slats flat side down onto the canvas between the guide strips as shown *below*.

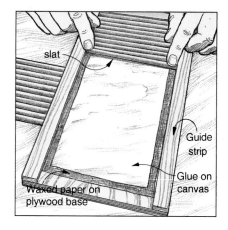

4. After laying the 24th tambour slat, position the remaining guide strip firmly against it, and tack it in place. Now, cut a piece of scrap large enough to fit over the tambour within the guide strips. Place it on top of the tambour slats and clamp it down to apply modest pressure to the tambour slots.

5. Remove the tambour from the gluing guide. If glue squeezed out and dried between the tambours, place it canvas side down on the edge of a bench, and carefully roll it over the edge to loosen the slats.

The final steps: finish and assemble

1. Dry-assemble the box by inserting the tenons along the edges of the bottom and back into the slots in the sides. Slide the tambour into side grooves and check the fit. Sand the underside of the tambour ends or tambour groove lightly if needed to make the tambour roll easily. Remove the tambour and glue the pull to the front slat. See the Tambour drawing at *right*. Trim the canvas edges.

2. Finish the tambour and the inside surfaces of the box. (After applying an oak stain, we masked the tenons and slots, applied a coat of water-based sanding sealer, and then two coats of water-based polyurethane. We rubbed each coat with a fine Scotchbrite pad.)

3. Remove the masking. Glue the bottom/back and sides together. Clamp, and square the box by measuring from side to side, and diagonally from the front to back. After the glue dries, remove the clamps. Finish the bar, the outside of the box, and the outside surface of the front piece, following the same procedures used on the inside.

4. Finish assembling the box by sliding the tambour into the groove. Now, glue the front piece in the slot, aligning the bottom edge with the bottom edges of the sides.

Project Tool List

Tablesaw
Bandsaw or scrollsaw
Belt sander
Router
  Router table
  Bits: ¼" straight, ⅛" round-over, ½" round-over
  Guide bushing, ½"
Drill press
  Bits: ⁷⁄₆₄", ⁵⁄₃₂", ¼", ¹⁷⁄₆₄"
Finishing sander

Note: *We built the project using the tools listed. You may be able to substitute other tools or equipment for listed items you don't have. Additional common hand tools and clamps may be required to complete the project.*

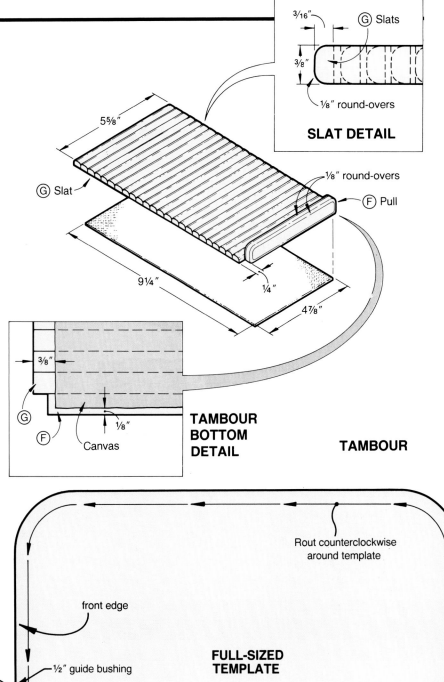

SLAT DETAIL

3/16" ⑤ Slats
3/8"
⅛" round-overs

⅛" round-overs
Ⓕ Pull
Ⓖ Slat
5⅝"
9¼"
¼"
4⅞"

TAMBOUR

Ⓖ
Ⓕ
3/8"
⅛"
Canvas

TAMBOUR BOTTOM DETAIL

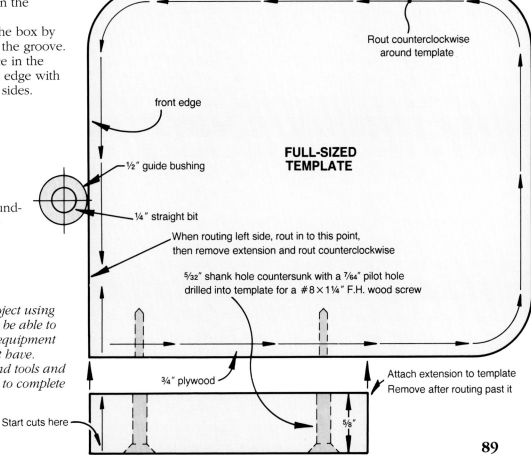

Rout counterclockwise around template

FULL-SIZED TEMPLATE

front edge

½" guide bushing

¼" straight bit

When routing left side, rout in to this point, then remove extension and rout counterclockwise

⁵⁄₃₂" shank hole countersunk with a ⁷⁄₆₄" pilot hole drilled into template for a #8 × 1¼" F.H. wood screw

Attach extension to template
Remove after routing past it

¾" plywood
5/8"

Start cuts here

PLANE PERPLEXING

A puzzled pilot? Heaven help us. But a plane puzzle—ah, that's something everyone can enjoy. This brainteaser wings its way from *WOOD*® magazine's Build-a-Toy™ contest. You'll appreciate the hours of design work Bruce Stevenson has put into this prize-winning toy.

Your first assignment: build the plane's fuselage

1. From ¾"-thick stock (we used walnut), rip and crosscut three 3×10" pieces. Laminate the pieces face-to-face and clamp. After the glue has dried, join one edge, and then rip the laminate to 2¼" square. Square one end of the blank, and then trim it to 9⅛" long. Now, scribe a centerline on each blank face front.

2. Photocopy the full-sized airplane patterns on *pages 94–96*, and cut out the four fuselage patterns. Adhere the Top, Bottom, and Left Side patterns to your blank, aligning the centerlines. (We used spray adhesive.) Turn the blank so the left side pattern faces up. Drill the ½"-diameter hole through the blank. Now, adhere the Right Side pattern to the blank, centering it on the ½" hole you just drilled, and aligning it with the centerlines on the blank.

3. Mark the centerpoints of all holes shown on the fuselage patterns. Drill these holes as dimensioned on the patterns. Bore the %₂" propeller hole 1¾" deep into the fuselage's front end as shown *below*.

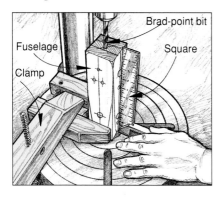

Brad-point bit

Fuselage

Square

Clamp

Note: For easier assembly, we used a ¹⁷⁄₆₄" bit to drill the holes where the ¼" dowels are glued. When the ¼" dowels must slide or turn, we enlarged the holes to %₂". To ensure accurate hole alignment, we first marked all hole centerpoints with an awl, and then drilled them with brad-point bits. When you do not have a brad-point bit in the exact size required, we suggest you first drill the hole with the closest smaller available brad-point bit. Then, redrill the holes with a proper-sized twist drill.

4. To bandsaw the fuselage (A), saw along the dashed lines on a side pattern to cut away the top and bottom as shown at *right*. Tape both scrap pieces back onto the blank. (We used double-faced tape for this.) Now, place the fuselage bottom side down, and then saw along the dashed lines of the top pattern to cut away the fuselage's sides.

5. Remove all of the scraps and tape from the fuselage. Next, sand all cut surfaces with 100-grit sandpaper to level the saw kerfs.

Chuck a ¼" piloted round-over bit into your table-mounted router, and round over all edges on the plane's fuselage. Now, finish-sand the fuselage with 180- and then 220-grit sandpaper.

Move on to the wings and tail

1. From ¾"-thick cherry (ours actually measured ¹³⁄₁₆"-thick), cut a 2⅞×12" piece for the wings and one 2×12" piece for the tail parts. Next, set your tablesaw's rip fence ¾" from the blade and then tilt your blade 5° from perpendicular. (We used our adjustable triangle to set the blade's angle accurately.) Bevel-

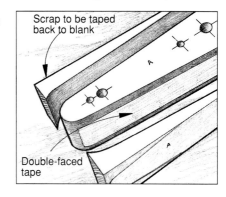

Scrap to be taped back to blank

Double-faced tape

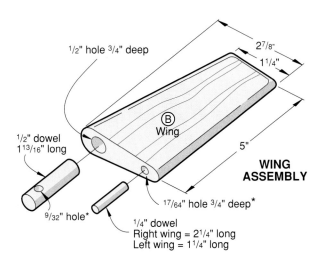

1/2" hole 3/4" deep

2 7/8"

1 1/4"

B
Wing

1/2" dowel
1 13/16" long

5"

**WING
ASSEMBLY**

9/32" hole*

1/4" dowel
Right wing = 2 1/4" long
Left wing = 1 1/4" long

17/64" hole 3/4" deep*

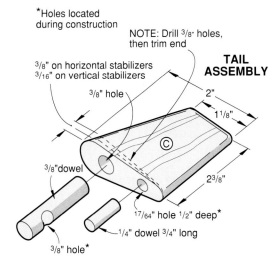

*Holes located
during construction

NOTE: Drill 3/8" holes,
then trim end

**TAIL
ASSEMBLY**

3/8" on horizontal stabilizers
3/16" on vertical stabilizers

3/8" hole

2"

1 1/8"

C

3/8" dowel

2 3/8"

3/8" hole

17/64" hole 1/2" deep*

1/4" dowel 3/4" long

3/8" hole*

rip one face of the wing blank. Now, tilt the saw blade 10°. Place the beveled side of the piece against the fence and wide edge down, and bevel-rip it again. Rip the tail blank the same way, setting the saw blade at 6° and 12° for the bevel cuts. Sand all sawed surfaces.

2. Crosscut two 5"-long wings (B) from the 2 7/8"-wide piece. Center the Left Wing End pattern on the end of one piece, and the Right Wing End pattern on the end of the second. Next, mark the 1/2"-hole centerpoints on the wing ends, and drill them 3/4" deep as shown *below*.

Note: *To ensure the dowels in the wings, canopy, and tail parts align with their mating holes in the fuselage, use the technique described in the next step to locate the hole centerpoints. We've identified these holes with an asterisk (*) on the drawings.*

3. To locate the 17/64" holes in the wings (and other parts too), first insert a 1" length of scrap 1/2" dowel in the 1/2" wing hole. Next, insert this dowel's free end into the appropriate mating fuselage hole. At

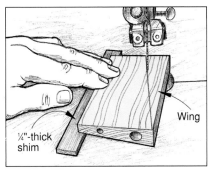

1/4"-thick
shim

Wing

the same time, place a 1/4" dowel center in the adjacent 9/32" fuselage hole, and then align the wing against the dowel center to mark the hole centerpoint on the wing end. Mark the second wing the same way. Drill these holes 3/4" deep into the wing ends following the same procedures used in Step 2.

4. Lay out the wings as shown *top left*. Saw both wings to shape as shown *above*. (We used a 1/4"-thick shim under the trailing edge of each wing to level it and keep the cut square to the leading edge.)

5. Crosscut the 2×12" piece into three 2 3/8" lengths. Name and mark the three tail parts. Next, adhere the Stabilizer End patterns to the end of the appropriate pieces, and then mark the centerpoints for the 3/8" holes. Now, drill these holes to the depth indicated on the patterns.

6. As shown on the Tail Assembly drawing *top right*, scribe a mark 3/8" from the end on the leading edge of both horizontal stabilizers, and 3/16" from the end on the vertical stabilizer. As shown

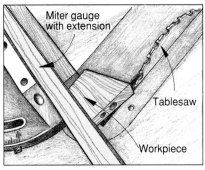

Miter gauge
with extension

Tablesaw

Workpiece

above, set your miter gauge to support the pieces, and miter-cut the ends of each at these marks.

7. Mark the 17/64" holes in the ends of the stabilizers, following the same procedure you used to mark the wing ends in Step 3. Now, drill these holes to the depth indicated on your patterns.

8. Lay out the three stabilizers, using the dimensions on the Tail Assembly drawing. Saw the three parts to shape, using the same techniques you used to shape the wings.

9. Set up your table-mounted router as shown on the Router Setup drawing *below*. Round over
continued

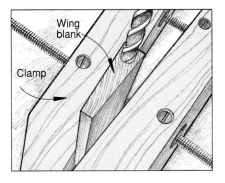

Wing
blank

Clamp

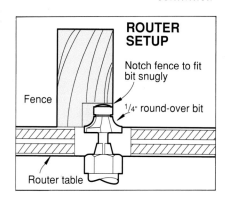

**ROUTER
SETUP**

Notch fence to fit
bit snugly

Fence

1/4" round-over bit

Router table

PLANE PERPLEXING
continued

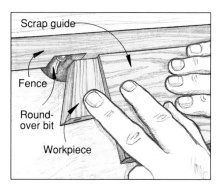

Scrap guide
Fence
Round-over bit
Workpiece

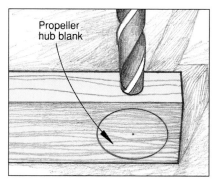

Propeller hub blank

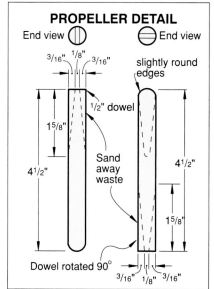

PROPELLER DETAIL

End view ◯ ◯ End view

3/16" 1/8" 3/16"

slightly round edges

1/2" dowel

1 5/8"

4 1/2"

Sand away waste

4 1/2"

1 5/8"

Dowel rotated 90°

3/16" 1/8" 3/16"

all edges on the wings and stabilizers except those that fit against the fuselage. (We used a piece of scrap to guide the tail parts safely past the router bit. See the drawing *above center.* You may sand the round-overs on these small pieces if you prefer.) Now, finish-sand the wings and tail parts, but do not reduce their thickness.

Now, prepare the canopy and landing gear

1. For the plane's canopy (D), laminate a 1¼×1½×4" cherry blank. Scribe a centerline along the bottom face and the ends. Locate the front ¹⁷⁄₆₄" hole centerpoint using the dimensions on the Canopy detail *opposite.* Drill the hole ¾" deep.

2. Adhere the Top and Side Canopy patterns to the blank, aligning the pattern centerlines with the centerline and front edge on the blank. Mark the two remaining holes in the canopy blank using dowel centers. Drill these holes ⅝" deep.

3. Saw the ⁵⁄₁₆" wedge-shaped piece from the bottom of the canopy blank (dashed line on the side pattern). Tape the cutoff piece back onto the blank. Turn the blank on its bottom, and then saw around the Top pattern outline. Remove the scrap and finish-sand the sawed surfaces. Sand the canopy to shape. (We sanded it on our stationary belt sander until we formed a shape we liked.)

4. Cut a ¾×¾×2" piece of cherry, and adhere the Front Landing Gear pattern to its top. Drill the ½"-diameter hole ³⁄₁₆" deep. Using dimensions on the Front Landing

Gear detail *opposite*, mark the centerpoint for the ⁹⁄₃₂" axle hole. Drill all the way through the piece. Next, mark the ¹⁷⁄₆₄" dowel hole in the top and drill it ³⁄₁₆" deep. Now, sand the front landing gear (E) to shape, and then remove the pattern.

5. Cut a ¾×¾×1⅜" cherry blank for the rear landing gear (F). Drill the ½" hole centered in the top where shown on the Rear Landing Gear detail, *opposite*. Locate and drill the ¹⁷⁄₆₄" hole and the ⁹⁄₃₂" axle hole.

6. To make the propeller hub (G), scribe a 1¼"-diameter circle on a ¾"-thick piece of cherry scrap. Using a try square, transfer the centerline of the circle down the side of the piece, mark the centerpoint along this line, and then drill a ½"-diameter hole through the blank as shown *above*. Drill a ¹⁷⁄₆₄" hole ³⁄₁₆" deep into the center of the circle. Now, cut out the 1¼"-diameter disc on your

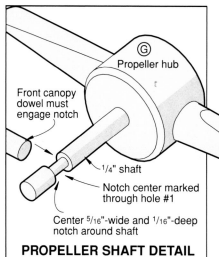

(G) Propeller hub

Front canopy dowel must engage notch

¼" shaft

Notch center marked through hole #1

Center 5/16"-wide and 1/16"-deep notch around shaft

PROPELLER SHAFT DETAIL

scrollsaw, sand it round, and round over the hub's front edge.

7. Crosscut a 4½" length of ½" walnut dowel for the propeller blade. Sand it to the shape shown on the Propeller detail *above*.

8. Insert the propeller into the hub, angle it 45° to the hub's front, and center it end to end. Redrill the existing ¹⁷⁄₆₄" hole in the hub center to ½" deep. Crosscut a 2¼" length of ¼" dowel and insert it into this hole.

You're nearly ready for the maiden flight

1. Crosscut ½" dowels for the wings and landing gear as dimensioned. Glue the dowels into the dowel holes in these parts. Chamfer the ends on all dowels except the wheel axles.

Note: The dowels must be specific lengths to make the interlocking parts. We cut them ¼" longer initially, and then trimmed them to correct length.

2. Crosscut ⅜"-diameter dowels for the tail parts. Glue them in the holes and trim to length. Cut ¼" dowels for the wings, tail parts, canopy, landing gear, and wheel axles. Glue them in the holes, and trim to length.

Note: The canopy dowels lock the propeller and wings to the fuselage. The propeller shaft locks the front

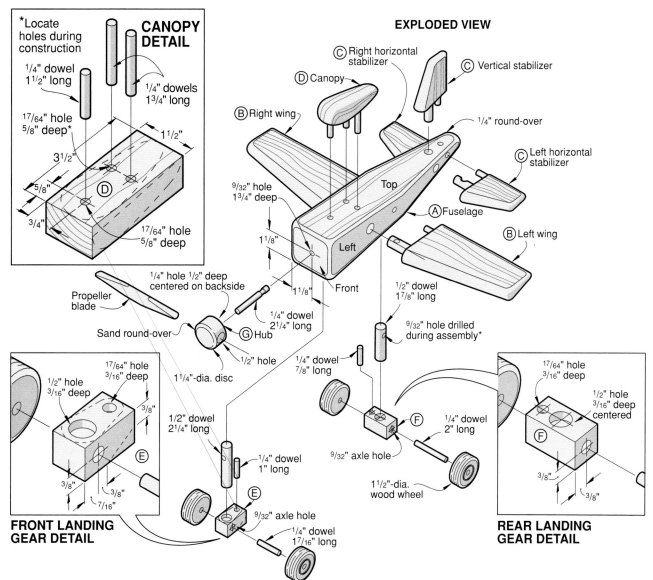

CANOPY DETAIL

EXPLODED VIEW

FRONT LANDING GEAR DETAIL

REAR LANDING GEAR DETAIL

landing gear, and the right wing locks the rear landing gear in place. The vertical stabilizer locks both horizontal stabilizers in the fuselage. To create these locks, drill through the numbered fuselage holes with the parts in place, as detailed in the next five steps.

3. Place the propeller shaft in the front fuselage hole. Insert a ¼" brad-point bit in hole #1 (see patterns for hole numbers) until it touches the propeller shaft. Apply pressure on the bit while turning the shaft to mark it. Remove the dowel shaft and then cut a ⁵⁄₁₆"-wide groove ¹⁄₁₆" deep around the shaft and centered on the mark as shown on the Propeller Shaft detail *opposite*. (We chucked the dowel in an electric hand drill and spun it while

holding the edge of a file against it.) Now, glue the shaft in the propeller hub, reinsert it in the fuselage hole, and then position your canopy on the fuselage to check the length of its front dowel. Shorten this dowel if necessary for a good fit in the propeller shaft's notch.

4. Remove the propeller. Position the front landing gear in the fuselage. Next, using a ⁹⁄₃₂" bit, drill into hole #2 and through the ½"-diameter landing-gear dowel.

5. Attach the wings to the fuselage. Now, using the same bit, drill through fuselage holes #3 and #4 to drill through the ½" wing dowels.

continued

Bill of Materials				
Part	**Finished Size***		**Mat.**	**Qty.**
	T	**W**	**L**		
A fuselage	2¼"	2¼"	9⅛"	W	1
B wing	¾"	2⅞"	5"	C	2
C tail	¾"	2"	2⅜"	C	3
D canopy	1¼"	1½"	3½"	C	1
E front gear	¾"	¾"	1⅝"	C	1
F rear gear	¾"	¾"	1⅜"	C	1
G hub	¾"	1¼" dia.		C	1

*All parts cut to final size during construction. Please read instructions before cutting.

Material Key: W—walnut; C—cherry
Supplies: ¼", ⅜", ½"-birch dowel, ½" walnut dowel, four 1½"-diameter wooden toy wheels.

PLANE PERPLEXING

continued

6. Remove the wings and attach the rear landing gear to the fuselage. Drill into fuselage hole #5 (right side) and through the ½" dowel of that landing gear.

7. Attach the horizontal stabilizers to the fuselage. With a ⅜" bit, carefully drill into hole #6 and through the ⅜" dowels of both horizontal stabilizers.

8. Finish-sand any parts needing touch up. Apply the finish of your choice. (We applied one coat of sanding sealer and two coats of polyurethane, sanding each coat after it dried with 320-grit sandpaper.) Glue and assemble the wheels and landing gear. Finally, assemble the airplane to complete the puzzle.

Project Tool List

Tablesaw
Bandsaw
Scrollsaw
Drill press
Portable drill
    Bits: ¹⁷⁄₆₄", ⁹⁄₃₂" , ⅜", ½"
Router
    Router table
    ¼" round-over bit
Finishing sander

Note: We built the project using the tools listed. You may be able to substitute other tools or equipment for listed items you don't have. Additional common hand tools and clamps may be required to complete the project.

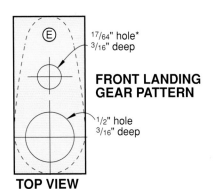

FRONT LANDING GEAR PATTERN

¹⁷⁄₆₄" hole*
³⁄₁₆" deep

½" hole
³⁄₁₆" deep

TOP VIEW

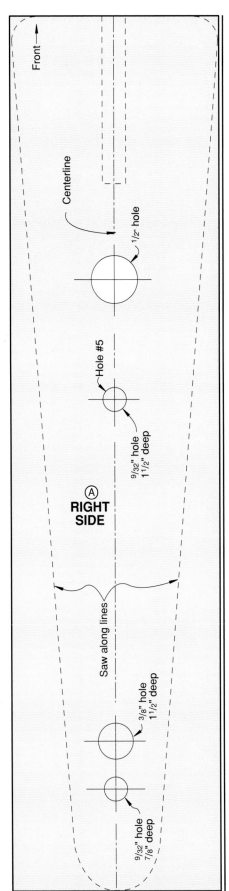

Front

Centerline

½" hole

Hole #5

⁹⁄₃₂" hole
1½" deep

Ⓐ **RIGHT SIDE**

Saw along lines

³⁄₈" hole
1½" deep

⁹⁄₃₂" hole
⅞" deep

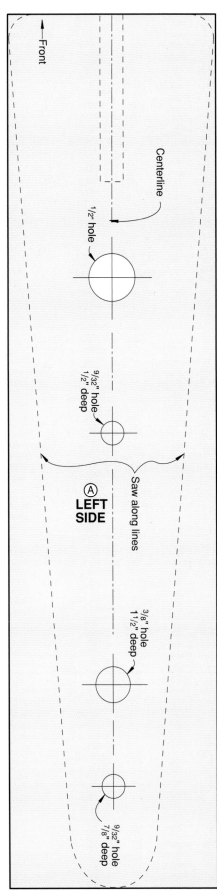

Front

Centerline

½" hole

⁹⁄₃₂" hole
½" deep

Saw along lines

³⁄₈" hole
1½" deep

⁹⁄₃₂" hole
⅞" deep

Ⓐ **LEFT SIDE**

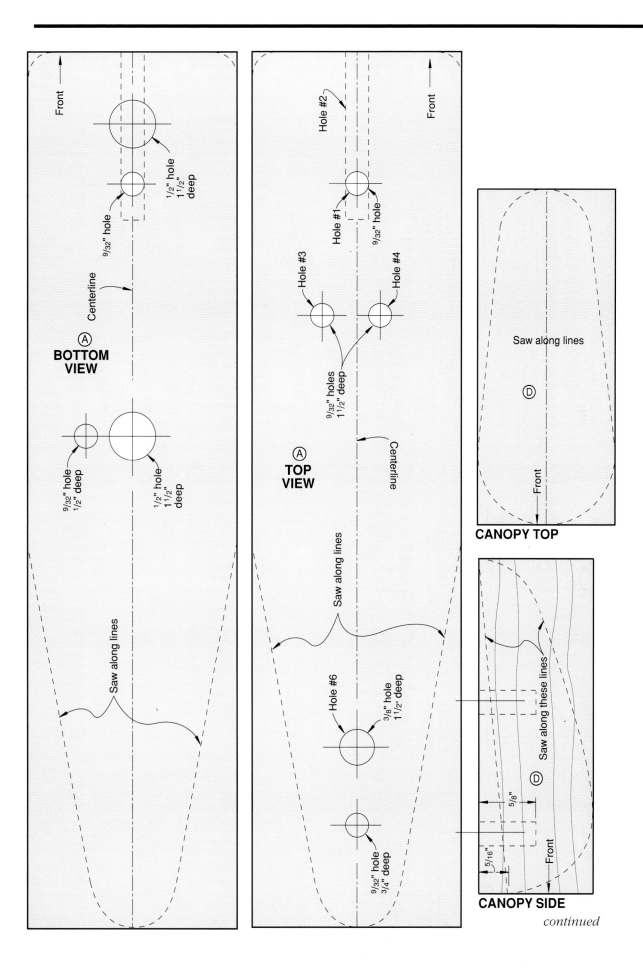

BOTTOM VIEW Ⓐ

Front

Centerline

1/2" hole 1 1/2" deep

9/32" hole

9/32" hole 1/2" deep

1/2" hole 1 1/2" deep

Saw along lines

TOP VIEW Ⓐ

Front

Hole #2

Hole #1

9/32" hole

Hole #3

Hole #4

9/32" holes 1 1/2" deep

Centerline

Saw along lines

Hole #6

3/8" hole 1 1/2" deep

9/32" hole 3/4" deep

CANOPY TOP

Saw along lines

Ⓓ

Front

CANOPY SIDE

Saw along these lines

Ⓓ

5/8"

5/16"

Front

continued

PLANE PERPLEXING

continued

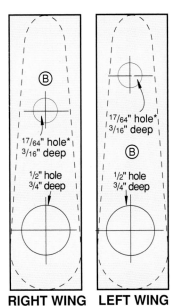

RIGHT WING **LEFT WING**

VERTICAL STABILIZER

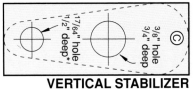

RIGHT HORIZ. STABILIZER

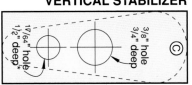

LEFT HORIZ. STABILIZER

ACKNOWLEDGMENTS

Writers

Larry Clayton—Basic Mortise and Tenon Joinery, pages 26–31

Roger W. Cliffe—How Your Choice of Router Bits Shapes Up, pages 12–14

James R. Downing—Five Great Router Tricks, pages 20–25; Tambour, pages 44–49

Bill Krier—Five Great Router Tricks, pages 20–25; Tambour, pages 44–49

Project Designers

Jim Boelling—Router Straightedge Makes Dadoes and Edge-Jointing a Snap, pages 16–17; Resplendent Pendant, pages 72–73

Gary Damaskos—Musical Tone Box, pages 82–85

V.W. Doyle—Tambouriffic Rolltop Recipe Box, pages 86–89
James R. Downing—Heavy-Duty Router Table, pages 5–11; Router Straightedge Makes Dadoes and Edge-Jointing a Snap, pages 16–17; Picture Perfect Parsons Table, pages 51–58; Mancala Marble Game, pages 68–71; Stylized Meat Carving Board, pages 74–77; Lazy Susan, pages 78–81

Bob Livingston—Christmas-Tree Tray, pages 59–62

Albert McCaffrey—Tea-for-Two Hutch, pages 63–67

Bruce Stevenson—Plane Perplexing, pages 90–96

Photographers

Bob Calmer
John Hetherington
Hopkins Associates
Jim Kascoutas
John Schultz

Illustrators

Advertising Arts Studios, Inc
James R. Downing
Jamie Downing
Kim Downing
Mike Henry
Roxanne LeMoine
Carson Ode
Ode Designs
Greg Roberts
Jim Stevenson
Bill Zaun

If you would like to order any additional copies of our books, call 1-800-678-2802 or check with your local bookstore.